I0829539

Get A Free Book At: https://free.xsputs.com

Table of Contents:

Hypnosis: An Introduction

Hypnosis is a trance-like state of focused attention and heightened suggestibility, often accompanied by deep relaxation. It has intrigued people for centuries, from ancient rituals to modern therapeutic practices. Contrary to popular belief, hypnosis is not a form of mind control or magical influence, but rather a state where an individual is more open to suggestions and can access a deeper level of their consciousness. This heightened suggestibility can be used for various purposes, including therapeutic interventions, self-improvement, and even entertainment.

In a clinical setting, hypnosis is often used to help individuals manage pain, reduce stress and anxiety, and address behavioral issues such as smoking or overeating. Through a process known as *hypnotherapy*, a trained therapist can guide a person into a state of deep relaxation, allowing them to focus intensely on particular thoughts or images, which can lead to significant changes in perception, emotion, or behavior. The mind, while in this suggestible state, is more capable of reshaping habits, managing psychological stress, or revisiting past memories.

One of the key aspects of hypnosis is that it doesn't work on everyone in the same way. While some individuals are highly susceptible and can easily enter a hypnotic state, others may find it difficult to achieve the same depth of relaxation or suggestibility. This variability can be influenced by factors such as personality, level of concentration, and even one's beliefs about hypnosis.

The history of hypnosis dates back to the 18th century when Franz Anton Mesmer, an Austrian physician, developed a theory called "animal magnetism," which was a precursor to modern hypnosis. While Mesmer's theories were later discredited, his ideas about the power of suggestion and focused attention laid the groundwork for future research. The term "hypnosis" itself comes from the Greek word *hypnos*, meaning "sleep," though it's important to note that hypnosis does not involve actual sleep. Instead, it is a state of focused awareness, often likened to daydreaming or deep meditation.

While hypnosis has gained recognition in medical and psychological fields, it still faces skepticism in some circles. Many misconceptions persist, especially in popular media, where hypnosis is portrayed as a form of mind control or as something that can force people to act against their will. In reality, individuals under hypnosis cannot be made to do anything that contradicts their moral beliefs or ethical standards. Instead, the experience is more about enhancing the mind's ability to concentrate and engage with specific thoughts, memories, or goals.

Although hypnosis has been largely associated with therapeutic applications, it is also widely used in entertainment, such as stage hypnosis. In these performances, a hypnotist invites volunteers from the audience to enter a trance state, where they may participate in humorous or unusual activities, often for the amusement of the crowd. While these performances are carefully controlled and scripted, they rely on the volunteers' willingness to engage in the process, rather than any coercion or manipulation.

In summary, hypnosis is a powerful tool for influencing the mind, capable of fostering positive change when applied therapeutically. While misconceptions abound, its true potential lies in its ability to help individuals tap into their subconscious minds to promote healing, self-improvement, and personal growth.

Defining Hypnosis

Hypnosis is a state of focused attention, heightened suggestibility, and deep relaxation, often accompanied by a sense of detachment from the external world. It is neither sleep nor unconsciousness, but rather a unique mental condition in which the individual's awareness is concentrated on a particular thought, sensation, or behavior. This state allows for more vivid imagination, enhanced perception, and increased openness to suggestions, making hypnosis a tool used for both therapeutic and personal development purposes.

At its core, hypnosis involves a process in which a person is guided into a trance-like state by a trained practitioner, often called a hypnotist or hypnotherapist. This induction can be achieved through various methods, such as verbal cues, relaxation techniques, or visualization exercises. Once the individual is deeply relaxed and focused, their subconscious mind becomes more accessible, allowing for targeted suggestions or therapeutic interventions.

Despite the popular myths, hypnosis is not about losing control or being "mind-controlled." People in a hypnotic state are not unconscious or asleep; they remain fully aware of their surroundings and can choose to reject any suggestion that conflicts with their values or desires. Hypnosis relies on the subject's willingness and ability to focus, meaning that not everyone can be easily hypnotized. Some individuals may be highly suggestible, while others may not enter the state as easily, which is often referred to as "hypnotic susceptibility."

In a therapeutic context, hypnosis, or *hypnotherapy*, can be used to address a variety of psychological and physical issues. It has been applied to manage chronic pain, reduce stress and anxiety, treat phobias, enhance performance, and even assist in behavior modification, such as smoking cessation or weight loss. The technique works by helping individuals access a relaxed state where they can reframe negative thought patterns, alter undesirable habits, or confront past traumas in a controlled, supportive manner.

Hypnosis is also linked to the concept of *suggestibility*, which refers to the individual's susceptibility to suggestions while in a trance-like state. While this does not mean that a person will act against their will or ethical beliefs, it does mean they are more likely to adopt new perspectives, behaviors, or attitudes that are presented to them during the hypnotic session. This quality makes hypnosis particularly useful in modifying certain behaviors, alleviating psychological distress, or improving mental well-being.

It's important to recognize that hypnosis is not a universal cure-all, and its effectiveness depends on various factors, including the skill of the practitioner, the nature of the issue being addressed, and the individual's openness to the process. Furthermore, while the scientific community generally acknowledges the therapeutic potential of hypnosis, it is still subject to ongoing research and debate, particularly regarding its mechanisms and long-term effectiveness.

In conclusion, hypnosis is a versatile and powerful tool for accessing the subconscious mind, enhancing personal growth, and addressing various psychological and physiological concerns. It remains a fascinating field, blending science, psychology, and therapeutic practice, and offers an intriguing way to explore the potential of the human mind.

The History of Hypnosis

The history of hypnosis stretches back centuries, evolving from ancient practices into the modern therapeutic tool we know today. Though the term "hypnosis" itself is relatively new, the concept of altered states of consciousness and suggestion can be traced through various cultures and belief systems.

One of the earliest recorded uses of hypnotic-like practices comes from ancient Egypt, Greece, and Rome, where priests and healers employed rituals involving chants, drumming, or other rhythmic activities to induce trance states. These techniques were often used for healing purposes, with individuals entering altered states to receive divine guidance or undergo therapeutic treatments. The word "sleep" was frequently associated with these trance-like states, even though individuals in these states were not truly unconscious.

In the 18th century, the origins of modern hypnosis began to take shape through the work of Franz Anton Mesmer, an Austrian physician. Mesmer proposed a theory called "animal magnetism," which suggested that an invisible force flowed through living beings, similar to a magnetic fluid. He believed this force could be manipulated to treat ailments, and he used techniques that involved touch and the use of magnets to "restore balance" to a person's body. While Mesmer's theories were eventually discredited, his work laid the groundwork for the study of hypnosis, as he recognized the powerful effects of suggestion and the mind-body connection.

Mesmer's ideas were further refined by figures such as James Braid, a Scottish surgeon who, in the early 19th century, began studying the phenomena more scientifically. Braid coined the term "hypnotism" in 1843, deriving it from the Greek word *hypnos* (sleep), though he was the first to clarify that hypnosis was not a form of sleep, but a heightened state of focus and concentration. He demonstrated that hypnosis could be induced without the use of magnets or other physical devices, shifting the practice away from mystical and pseudo-scientific interpretations and towards a more psychological understanding.

In the late 19th and early 20th centuries, hypnosis gained recognition as a therapeutic tool. Sigmund Freud, the father of psychoanalysis, experimented with hypnosis to explore the unconscious mind, though he later abandoned it in favor of free association. However, the work of French neurologist Jean-Martin Charcot at the Salpêtrière Hospital in Paris significantly influenced the medical and psychological communities. Charcot used hypnosis to treat hysteria and other psychological disorders, presenting it as a legitimate tool for understanding the mind.

During the same period, the development of *hypnotherapy*—the use of hypnosis for therapeutic purposes—was gaining traction. Hypnotists like Milton Erickson in the mid-20th century became pioneers in using hypnosis to address mental health issues, such as anxiety, depression, and behavioral problems. Erickson, in particular, emphasized the importance of the therapeutic relationship between the hypnotist and the subject, as well as the creative and individualistic nature of hypnosis. His methods greatly influenced modern hypnotherapy techniques.

Throughout the 20th and 21st centuries, hypnosis became more widely accepted in both medical and psychological fields. It was increasingly used for pain management, stress reduction, and behavior modification. Clinical hypnosis, or *hypnotherapy*, was incorporated into mainstream psychological practices, and scientific research continued to explore its mechanisms and effectiveness. The American Psychological Association (APA) officially recognized hypnosis as a legitimate therapeutic technique, though ongoing studies continue to examine its scope and limitations.

In recent years, hypnosis has also gained popularity outside of the clinical realm, with stage hypnotism and entertainment playing a significant role in shaping public perceptions. While often dramatized for theatrical effect, stage hypnosis relies on the same basic principles of suggestion and focused attention as clinical hypnosis, though with a different goal—entertainment rather than therapy.

From its mystical and ritualistic origins to its modern-day applications in psychology and medicine, the history of hypnosis reflects humanity's long-standing interest in the power of the mind and its ability to influence physical and emotional well-being. As research continues and the practice evolves, hypnosis remains an intriguing and useful tool for understanding the complexities of human consciousness.

Misconceptions about Hypnosis

Hypnosis is often surrounded by misconceptions, many of which stem from its portrayal in popular media and its early associations with mysticism. One of the most common myths is that hypnosis is a form of mind control, where the hypnotist can make people do things against their will. In reality, individuals under hypnosis cannot be coerced into actions that contradict their ethical beliefs or personal values. While hypnosis can increase suggestibility, it does not override a person's moral compass or ability to make conscious decisions.

Another prevalent misconception is that hypnosis is equivalent to sleep. The term itself, derived from the Greek word *hypnos* (meaning sleep), contributes to this misunderstanding. However, hypnosis is a distinct state of heightened awareness and focused concentration, not unconsciousness. People who are hypnotized are not asleep— they remain fully aware of their surroundings and can often recall everything that occurs during the session. It is more akin to a deep daydream or focused meditation, where the mind is intensely concentrated but not in a sleep-like state.

A third myth is the belief that only certain people can be hypnotized, and that others are immune to the process. While it is true that some individuals are more susceptible to hypnosis than others, almost everyone can be hypnotized to some extent. The depth of hypnosis a person can achieve may vary based on factors such as concentration, willingness, and trust in the process, but even individuals with low susceptibility can experience mild hypnotic states that can still be beneficial. Hypnosis is not a magical skill reserved for a select few but a natural phenomenon that can be cultivated with practice and guidance.

Hypnosis is also often mistakenly thought to be a quick fix for complex issues. While it can be highly effective for certain problems, such as pain management, stress reduction, or habit change, it is not a one-time solution for deep-seated psychological issues. In therapeutic contexts, hypnosis is often used in conjunction with other forms of treatment, and long-term results usually require sustained effort, follow-up sessions, and sometimes additional therapies.

Some people believe that hypnosis is dangerous or harmful, fearing that they could lose control or experience lasting negative effects. However, hypnosis is generally considered safe when practiced by trained professionals. It has been extensively researched and used in clinical settings with positive results. The process itself is non-invasive, and any potential risks are minimal when proper protocols are followed. People under hypnosis cannot be made to do anything that would harm them or put them in a dangerous situation.

Another myth is that hypnosis can bring about superhuman feats or reveal hidden memories. While hypnosis can enhance concentration and may allow individuals to access deeper levels of awareness, it cannot unlock extraordinary abilities or uncover repressed memories with perfect accuracy. The memories retrieved under hypnosis can sometimes be distorted or influenced by suggestion, and not all hypnotic "memories" are reliable. Moreover, using hypnosis to recover repressed memories is controversial and has led to debates within the mental health community due to the potential for false memories.

Finally, some individuals believe that hypnosis is only used for entertainment, often imagining it as a party trick or stage show where volunteers perform amusing or absurd acts. While stage hypnosis can be entertaining, it is based on the same principles as therapeutic hypnosis, relying on the subject's willingness to participate and focus. The key difference lies in the intention: entertainment hypnosis seeks to engage an audience, while therapeutic hypnosis aims to improve well-being and address personal issues.

In conclusion, hypnosis is a powerful and legitimate tool for therapeutic and personal development, but it is often misunderstood. It is not a form of mind control, nor is it synonymous with sleep. It is accessible to almost everyone, and while it can be highly effective, it is not a cure-all. When practiced by trained professionals, hypnosis is safe and can offer real benefits for those seeking to improve their mental and physical health.

Hypnosis and the Conscious Mind

Hypnosis is a process that involves altering the state of consciousness, allowing the mind to enter a focused, relaxed, and highly suggestible state. While the unconscious mind plays a central role in hypnosis, the conscious mind remains active throughout the process, interacting with the suggestions being presented. Understanding the relationship between hypnosis and the conscious mind can help clarify how hypnosis works and why it can be so effective for certain therapeutic purposes.

In our everyday experience, the conscious mind is responsible for logic, reasoning, and awareness. It is the part of the mind that processes immediate thoughts and sensations, directs attention, and makes decisions based on the information available in the present moment. This mental state allows us to navigate the world, solve problems, and manage tasks. However, the conscious mind is also limited in its ability to process large amounts of information simultaneously, often filtering out details that might be irrelevant or unimportant at any given time.

When a person enters a hypnotic state, the conscious mind becomes less dominant. Hypnosis involves the induction of deep relaxation and focused attention, which allows the conscious mind to quieten and let go of distractions. This shift in awareness opens the door for the subconscious mind to become more accessible. In this state, the mind becomes more open to suggestions, and the conscious filters that typically govern thoughts and behaviors are relaxed, which allows the individual to focus more deeply on specific thoughts or ideas presented by the hypnotist.

Despite the reduced dominance of the conscious mind during hypnosis, it is never fully shut off or rendered passive. The conscious mind remains aware of the process, often acting as a sort of observer or filter. For example, an individual under hypnosis might still be able to hear the hypnotist's voice, respond to questions, or remember what happens during the session. This awareness ensures that the subject is not under total control, and that they can engage with the process on their terms. The conscious mind may even play an active role in helping the individual accept or reject certain suggestions.

One of the key aspects of hypnosis is the ability to bypass the critical, analytical thinking of the conscious mind. In a normal state, the conscious mind tends to be more skeptical or cautious about new ideas or suggestions. However, during hypnosis, the critical thinking part of the mind becomes less active, allowing ideas that might normally be resisted to take root in the subconscious. This is why hypnosis is often used for behavior change—

such as overcoming a fear or breaking a bad habit—by presenting positive suggestions that can gradually replace negative thought patterns.

The conscious mind, however, is still integral to the process. For example, the person being hypnotized must be willing to enter the hypnotic state and cooperate with the process. Hypnosis cannot force someone to act against their will or values. Even though the conscious mind is more relaxed, it still serves as a safeguard, ensuring that the person remains in control of the experience and can terminate the session if they choose to do so. Additionally, the conscious mind is responsible for setting intentions for the session—whether it's for relaxation, self-improvement, or addressing a specific issue.

Hypnosis can also be used to heighten the effectiveness of conscious mental states. For example, individuals can use self-hypnosis techniques to improve concentration, enhance creativity, or reduce stress. In these cases, the conscious mind helps guide the individual through the process, but the deep relaxation and focus induced by hypnosis enhance the mental state, allowing the person to access deeper levels of concentration or insight.

In conclusion, while hypnosis primarily engages the subconscious mind, the conscious mind still plays a significant role in the process. It is the conscious mind that allows individuals to enter hypnosis in the first place and to maintain a sense of awareness throughout the experience. By reducing the dominance of the conscious mind's critical thinking, hypnosis allows for the more suggestible, creative, and solution-oriented aspects of the mind to take the lead, facilitating positive change and growth.

Understanding Consciousness

Consciousness is the state of being aware of and able to think about one's own existence, thoughts, and surroundings. It is a complex and multifaceted phenomenon, central to human experience, yet it remains one of the most debated topics in psychology, neuroscience, and philosophy. Understanding consciousness is crucial to understanding how the mind works, particularly when exploring altered states of consciousness, such as those induced by hypnosis.

At its core, consciousness can be divided into two broad categories: *awareness* and *wakefulness*. Awareness refers to the ability to perceive internal and external stimuli, while wakefulness refers to the brain's state of being awake and alert. These two aspects of consciousness work together, allowing individuals to experience thoughts, emotions, and sensory inputs. However, consciousness is not just about being aware of what is happening around us—it also involves the ability to reflect on those experiences, analyze them, and integrate them into a coherent understanding of the world.

In its normal state, consciousness operates on a level of heightened attention and awareness, where individuals process sensory information, make decisions, and engage in cognitive tasks. But consciousness is far from a static experience. It is constantly shifting, influenced by emotions, sensory inputs, and cognitive processes. One of the most interesting aspects of consciousness is its capacity for *self-awareness*, the ability to not only perceive the world but to reflect on one's own thoughts and existence. This metacognitive ability allows humans to think about their thoughts, question their experiences, and even alter their perspectives.

In the context of hypnosis, consciousness is altered in a controlled way. While an individual is in a hypnotic state, their conscious awareness does not disappear, but it becomes focused and more selective. During hypnosis, individuals can enter a state of deep concentration, where they may feel detached from their surroundings and less aware of distractions. This focused state of awareness makes the subconscious mind more accessible and receptive to suggestions. Essentially, hypnosis temporarily shifts the balance between the conscious and subconscious minds, allowing for deeper exploration of internal thoughts and feelings.

The brain plays a key role in shaping consciousness. Neural activity, particularly in areas like the prefrontal cortex and the thalamus, is involved in maintaining a waking consciousness, processing sensory information, and facilitating higher cognitive functions such as reasoning and decision-making. When an individual enters hypnosis, brainwave patterns shift, often moving from the faster, beta waves associated with active thinking, to slower alpha or theta waves, which are more associated with relaxation and deep focus. This shift in brainwave activity reflects the change in consciousness, allowing the hypnotized individual to enter a state of heightened suggestibility and introspection, but without losing full awareness of their environment.

It's important to note that the conscious mind does not simply "shut off" during hypnosis, as is often depicted in movies or popular media. Rather, it becomes less dominant, allowing the subconscious to become more engaged. This shift can enhance creativity, facilitate behavioral changes, and promote therapeutic healing. The conscious mind still plays an active role in ensuring that the suggestions provided during hypnosis are not contrary to the individual's values or desires.

One of the most fascinating aspects of consciousness is its fluidity and the potential for it to be altered in various ways. Altered states of consciousness, such as those induced by hypnosis, meditation, or even certain substances, provide unique opportunities to explore the mind's deeper layers. These altered states can reveal insights into unconscious thoughts, behaviors, and patterns that may not be accessible during normal waking consciousness. They offer a glimpse into the complexity of human cognition and the underlying processes that influence our thoughts and actions.

In conclusion, consciousness is an intricate and dynamic aspect of the human mind that shapes how we experience the world and ourselves. While it operates on a conscious, waking level, it also involves deeper layers that can be accessed and influenced through techniques like hypnosis. By understanding consciousness and how it can be altered, we can better appreciate the vast potential of the mind and explore its capacity for self-awareness, healing, and transformation.

Role of Hypnosis in Modifying Consciousness

Hypnosis plays a unique role in modifying consciousness, allowing individuals to access altered states of awareness that are different from their everyday experiences. In its essence, hypnosis is a tool that helps shift the balance between the conscious and subconscious minds. It creates a state of focused attention, heightened suggestibility, and deep relaxation, during which the usual filtering mechanisms of the conscious mind become less dominant. This enables the subconscious mind to become more accessible, offering opportunities for therapeutic change, self-improvement, and deeper exploration of the mind.

During hypnosis, the individual enters a trance-like state where their conscious awareness is significantly narrowed. This doesn't mean they are asleep or unconscious—rather, the mind becomes highly concentrated on specific thoughts, sensations, or suggestions. As the conscious mind becomes less active in processing irrelevant stimuli, the subconscious mind, which typically operates below the surface of awareness, becomes more receptive to new ideas and suggestions. This shift is akin to a heightened state of focus, similar to the deep concentration one experiences during intense meditation or while engaged in a creative flow state.

One of the key effects of hypnosis on consciousness is its ability to bypass the usual critical, analytical filters of the conscious mind. In normal waking consciousness, we constantly evaluate and assess incoming information, often rejecting or questioning new ideas that don't align with our beliefs or experiences. However, when an individual is hypnotized, the conscious mind's critical thinking and skepticism are relaxed, allowing suggestions to enter the subconscious more easily. This ability to access the subconscious makes hypnosis particularly effective for modifying behaviors, altering thought patterns, and even addressing deeply ingrained emotional issues like fear, anxiety, or self-doubt.

For example, in hypnotherapy, individuals seeking to overcome a fear or phobia may be guided into a relaxed, focused state, where they are encouraged to visualize situations that normally trigger anxiety, but in a controlled and safe manner. The therapist may then introduce suggestions that reframe the fearful experience or encourage more positive associations, helping to change the individual's emotional response. By altering the way the subconscious mind processes these triggers, hypnosis can lead to lasting changes in behavior and perception.

Hypnosis also has the capacity to modify awareness in ways that facilitate deeper self-exploration. Through focused introspection, individuals can access memories or thoughts that may be hidden or repressed in their waking state. While hypnosis does not "uncover" repressed memories with absolute accuracy, it can provide a platform for exploring past experiences, reframing old narratives, or gaining new insights into personal issues. This altered state of consciousness offers a safe space for individuals to explore emotions or memories that may be difficult to confront in a fully conscious state.

The relaxation induced by hypnosis also affects consciousness in ways that promote healing and stress reduction. When the conscious mind is relaxed and not constantly processing external stimuli or worries, the body enters a state of deep relaxation that can lower blood pressure, reduce stress hormones, and promote physical healing. This is why hypnosis is often used in medical settings for pain management, helping patients to alter their perception of pain or anxiety, and even reduce the need for anesthesia in some cases.

Moreover, hypnosis can improve the functioning of the conscious mind in certain areas. For instance, athletes or individuals seeking to improve their performance in a specific area often use hypnosis to enhance focus, concentration, and mental clarity. By altering the consciousness to create a heightened sense of concentration, hypnosis can help individuals achieve peak performance by eliminating distractions and improving their ability to visualize success or practice skills more effectively.

The role of hypnosis in modifying consciousness goes beyond just therapeutic purposes—it can also enhance creativity and problem-solving. By quieting the analytical mind, hypnosis allows the creative subconscious to come to the forefront, offering new ideas or solutions that may not be immediately accessible during ordinary states of consciousness. This is why some individuals use hypnosis to boost creativity, whether for artistic endeavors, writing, or overcoming mental blocks.

In summary, hypnosis is a powerful tool for modifying consciousness, offering a range of benefits that span from therapeutic applications to personal growth and enhanced creativity. By inducing a focused, relaxed state where the conscious mind's usual filters are reduced, hypnosis allows individuals to access deeper layers of their mind, enabling lasting behavioral change, emotional healing, and cognitive improvement. Whether used for therapy, performance enhancement, or self-exploration, hypnosis remains a valuable method for exploring and modifying the intricate landscape of human consciousness.

Conscious Mind: The Gatekeeper

The conscious mind serves as the gatekeeper of our mental landscape, regulating what enters our awareness and deciding how we respond to external stimuli. It is the part of the mind responsible for active thought processes, reasoning, and decision-making. Operating at the level of everyday awareness, the conscious mind constantly analyzes, filters, and evaluates information, ensuring that we stay alert, rational, and in control of our actions. However, its role as a gatekeeper is not absolute—particularly when we enter altered states of consciousness, such as hypnosis.

In normal, waking consciousness, the conscious mind plays a crucial role in managing the flow of information. It assesses what is important, discards irrelevant details, and focuses attention on the tasks at hand. This ability to filter out distractions helps us navigate the world and make decisions based on logical reasoning and experience. However, the conscious mind is limited by cognitive resources and can only process a small amount of information at a time. In this state, we are generally aware of only a fraction of the sensory and emotional inputs that shape our experience.

When hypnosis occurs, the conscious mind's role as the gatekeeper is temporarily relaxed. During hypnosis, an individual enters a deeply focused state of awareness where they are highly concentrated but relaxed. This shift reduces the filtering capacity of the conscious mind, allowing the subconscious to become more accessible. The usual defenses, such as skepticism, resistance, and critical thinking, are minimized, creating an environment where suggestions can bypass the conscious mind's normal skepticism and be absorbed more readily by the subconscious.

The conscious mind, however, is never fully absent during hypnosis. It remains aware of what is happening and can still exert control over the process. In fact, the ability to engage with hypnosis is dependent on the conscious mind's willingness to cooperate. A person cannot be hypnotized against their will or made to do anything that goes against their values or beliefs. The conscious mind, even in a relaxed state, is always present to ensure that the process remains safe and aligned with the individual's desires.

This dynamic interplay between the conscious and subconscious minds is central to how hypnosis works. The conscious mind is the logical, analytical part of the psyche, focused on reality and the present moment. In contrast, the subconscious mind operates more freely, processing emotions, memories, and automatic behaviors that are not immediately accessible to conscious thought. Hypnosis provides a way to temporarily shift the balance, allowing the subconscious to take center stage while the conscious mind takes a step back.

The conscious mind's role as a gatekeeper is especially important in therapeutic contexts. For example, in hypnotherapy, a person may enter a relaxed state where their critical thinking is softened, but they still retain the ability to assess the suggestions being offered. In this state, a therapist may guide the individual to address deep-seated fears, phobias, or behavioral issues, offering positive suggestions that the subconscious mind is more likely to accept. Since the conscious mind is less critical in this state, the individual can more easily reframe negative thought patterns and create lasting change.

In addition, the conscious mind often serves as a repository for a person's beliefs, memories, and learned behaviors. As a result, it can become cluttered with past experiences and emotional baggage, which may hinder personal growth or lead to self-sabotaging behaviors. Hypnosis allows the individual to bypass the conscious mind's usual defenses and delve deeper into the subconscious, where these deeper issues reside. Through suggestion and relaxation, the conscious mind's usual resistance can be softened, allowing for new insights, healing, and transformation.

While the conscious mind's filtering and protective functions are essential for navigating day-to-day life, its role can also create mental blocks or reinforce negative patterns. This is why hypnosis can be particularly effective in helping people overcome limitations. For example, by lowering the resistance of the conscious mind, hypnosis can help individuals break free from habits, reduce stress, or reprogram limiting beliefs. In this sense, the conscious mind is both the protector and the potential obstacle. Its role as gatekeeper is vital in keeping us grounded in reality, but when it comes to personal transformation, allowing it to step aside temporarily can open the door to new possibilities.

In conclusion, the conscious mind acts as the mental gatekeeper, filtering information and guiding our responses to the world around us. While it is crucial for maintaining logical thought, focus, and decision-making in everyday life, its role can limit access to deeper layers of the mind. Hypnosis, by temporarily relaxing the conscious mind's control, enables the subconscious to be more accessible for personal growth, behavioral change, and therapeutic healing. The dynamic relationship between the conscious and subconscious minds is essential for understanding how hypnosis can modify thoughts, behaviors, and perceptions, helping individuals overcome challenges and unlock new potential.

Hypnosis and the Subconscious Mind

The subconscious mind is a powerful and often overlooked aspect of human consciousness. While the conscious mind is responsible for our immediate awareness and decision-making, the subconscious operates largely beneath the surface, influencing thoughts, emotions, memories, and automatic behaviors without our active awareness. Hypnosis plays a significant role in accessing and influencing the subconscious, making it a valuable tool for therapeutic change and personal transformation.

In a typical state of consciousness, the subconscious mind is not directly accessible to the conscious mind. It functions in the background, storing memories, beliefs, habits, and emotional responses. These subconscious processes govern much of our behavior, influencing reactions and decisions based on past experiences or ingrained patterns. For example, when an individual has a phobia of spiders, it is often the result of a deeply embedded memory or learned fear stored in the subconscious mind. These subconscious memories and beliefs can shape how we view the world and respond to situations, even if we are unaware of their influence.

Hypnosis provides a means of bypassing the conscious mind's usual filters, allowing direct access to the subconscious. When a person enters a hypnotic state, their conscious mind becomes more relaxed and less focused on external distractions. This state of heightened concentration and deep relaxation enables the subconscious mind to become more receptive to suggestions and ideas. In this state, individuals are often able to access deeper memories, emotions, and automatic thought patterns that are normally hidden from their conscious awareness.

During hypnosis, the therapist can guide the individual to address subconscious issues, such as past trauma, unhealthy beliefs, or unwanted behaviors. Because the conscious mind's critical faculties are relaxed during hypnosis, it is easier to reframe or alter these deeply ingrained patterns. For example, a person who struggles with anxiety might be guided through a process that helps them reprogram their subconscious response to stressful situations, replacing anxiety with calmness and confidence.

One of the unique aspects of hypnosis is its ability to influence the subconscious in ways that the conscious mind might resist. In our waking state, the conscious mind often filters new information based on existing beliefs and judgments. This filtering mechanism can make it difficult to change established behaviors or thought patterns. However, hypnosis temporarily suspends this filtering process, allowing the individual to accept new suggestions and perspectives that may not be possible in a fully awake state. This makes hypnosis particularly effective for overcoming habits, phobias, and emotional blocks that are deeply rooted in the subconscious mind.

The subconscious mind also plays a key role in healing and self-improvement. Hypnotherapy has been used to help individuals manage chronic pain, reduce stress, and overcome sleep disorders, among other issues. By accessing the subconscious, hypnosis can help alter the perception of pain, alleviate anxiety, or encourage more positive, healing behaviors. In these cases, the subconscious mind is able to make adjustments to how the body experiences physical sensations or processes emotions, leading to lasting improvements in well-being.

In addition to addressing negative patterns, hypnosis can also enhance positive qualities stored in the subconscious mind. For example, a person seeking to boost their self-confidence may undergo hypnosis to strengthen their belief in their abilities. Positive affirmations and visualizations during hypnosis can help create new, empowering beliefs that replace old, limiting ones. By working directly with the subconscious, hypnosis can help individuals manifest desired changes in their lives, whether in terms of emotional well-being, physical health, or personal success.

Moreover, the subconscious mind is also responsible for creativity and problem-solving. Many individuals find that they experience breakthroughs or new insights during or after hypnosis. This is because the relaxed, focused state of hypnosis allows the subconscious mind to present new ideas, solutions, or perspectives that are not immediately accessible in a normal, conscious state. In this sense, hypnosis can be a valuable tool for enhancing creativity, decision-making, and innovation.

In summary, hypnosis provides a unique and powerful way to access and influence the subconscious mind. By relaxing the conscious mind's filtering mechanisms, hypnosis enables individuals to tap into deeper layers of the psyche, where memories, beliefs, emotions, and automatic behaviors reside. This access allows for the reprogramming of harmful patterns, the resolution of deep-seated issues, and the enhancement of personal growth. Whether used for therapeutic purposes or self-improvement, hypnosis offers a pathway to unlock the vast potential of the subconscious mind, leading to lasting change and transformation.

What is the Subconscious Mind?

The subconscious mind is a vast and largely hidden part of our mental landscape, operating beneath the surface of conscious awareness. It stores everything we experience, from memories and beliefs to habits and automatic behaviors. While we may not be actively aware of its influence, the subconscious plays a critical role in shaping how we think, feel, and behave. In the context of hypnosis, understanding the nature of the subconscious is key to grasping how this powerful tool can facilitate personal change, healing, and growth.

Unlike the conscious mind, which is responsible for immediate awareness, decision-making, and logical thought, the subconscious mind functions outside of our direct awareness. It operates automatically, managing tasks and processes that do not require conscious thought. For instance, when you drive a car, much of the action—such as steering, shifting gears, or checking mirrors—becomes automatic, handled by the subconscious. Likewise, your habitual responses to stress, anger, or joy are largely shaped by subconscious programming that has developed over time.

The subconscious mind is also the storage space for memories, both recent and distant, and influences how we react to stimuli based on past experiences. It holds the emotional content of memories, such as trauma or joy, and governs automatic reactions to certain triggers. For example, if someone has had a negative experience with a dog in childhood, their subconscious may cause them to feel anxious or fearful when they encounter a dog again, even if they don't consciously remember the original event. The subconscious mind not only stores these memories but also reinforces emotional patterns associated with them, even if the person is unaware of the underlying cause.

One of the defining features of the subconscious is its ability to create and reinforce habits. Habits, whether good or bad, are rooted in subconscious processes. For example, a person may subconsciously reach for a cigarette or sugary snack during moments of stress, even if they consciously know that these behaviors are not healthy. These automatic responses are often learned over time and stored in the subconscious mind. This is where hypnosis comes into play—by accessing the subconscious, it becomes possible to modify, replace, or eliminate such behaviors.

The subconscious also influences our beliefs and perceptions of ourselves and the world around us. Many of the core beliefs that guide our daily actions are formed early in life and become ingrained in the subconscious. These beliefs may relate to self-worth, success, love, or fear. For example, someone who was told repeatedly in childhood that they were not good enough may carry this belief into adulthood, shaping their behavior, relationships, and overall sense of self-worth. Hypnosis can help bring these subconscious beliefs to the surface, where they can be examined, reframed, or replaced with more empowering alternatives.

In addition to holding memories and beliefs, the subconscious mind is also a key player in managing emotions. It processes feelings that may be too overwhelming or repressed for the conscious mind to handle directly. Emotions like fear, anger, sadness, and joy are often stored in the subconscious and can influence our behavior, even if we're not consciously aware of them. Hypnosis allows individuals to access these emotional patterns, providing a way to process and release old, stuck emotions in a therapeutic setting.

The subconscious mind is also where creativity and intuition originate. Often, our most creative ideas and solutions come not from logical analysis, but from sudden insights or inspiration that arise seemingly out of nowhere. This is the subconscious mind at work—processing information in the background and offering up new possibilities when the conscious mind is distracted or at rest. This is one of the reasons why individuals often experience bursts of creativity or problem-solving insights during or after hypnosis.

Hypnosis can be a powerful tool for accessing and reshaping the subconscious mind. In a hypnotic state, the conscious mind becomes relaxed and less dominant, allowing the subconscious to come forward and become more receptive to new suggestions. This state of focused attention helps individuals confront deeply rooted beliefs, emotions, or habits that may be holding them back. By using hypnosis to directly influence the subconscious, individuals can replace negative behaviors, reframe limiting beliefs, and process unresolved emotions, leading to lasting changes in their mental and emotional well-being.

In summary, the subconscious mind is a fundamental aspect of human psychology that operates beneath our conscious awareness, controlling automatic behaviors, storing memories and emotions, and shaping our beliefs and habits. While the conscious mind handles immediate thought and decision-making, the subconscious mind governs deeper, more automatic processes that influence our daily lives. Through hypnosis, it is possible to access and modify the subconscious, facilitating profound personal transformation and growth. By understanding the power and role of the subconscious, we can better appreciate how hypnosis can be used to unlock its potential for healing, change, and self-improvement.

Accessing the Subconscious Through Hypnosis

Hypnosis is a powerful tool for accessing the subconscious mind, allowing individuals to bypass the usual filtering and critical functions of the conscious mind. In a hypnotic state, the conscious mind becomes relaxed and less focused on external distractions, creating an environment where the subconscious becomes more receptive to suggestions. This process allows people to access deeper layers of thought, emotion, and memory, often unlocking hidden insights and potential for change.

When a person enters hypnosis, they typically experience a deep state of relaxation and heightened focus. In this altered state of consciousness, the mind is not asleep or unconscious, but rather in a state of focused attention, similar to the mental state one might experience when deeply engrossed in a book or a movie. The conscious mind, which normally serves as a filter, becomes less active, allowing for easier access to the subconscious mind. It is in this state that suggestions, memories, emotions, and behaviors stored in the subconscious can be accessed, explored, and altered.

One of the key aspects of hypnosis is its ability to bypass the critical, logical thinking of the conscious mind. Normally, the conscious mind constantly evaluates and analyzes incoming information, often rejecting ideas or suggestions that do not align with existing beliefs or experiences. However, during hypnosis, the mind becomes more open and less resistant, which allows for the introduction of new thoughts or perspectives. This is especially useful in therapeutic settings, where individuals seek to modify unhealthy behaviors, beliefs, or emotional responses that are deeply rooted in the subconscious.

Through hypnosis, individuals can explore memories that may be buried or repressed in the subconscious. These memories can sometimes be linked to unresolved emotions or past trauma that continue to affect current behaviors and emotional responses. Hypnosis creates a safe environment for accessing these memories, allowing individuals to confront and process them in a controlled, therapeutic way. For example, someone dealing with a phobia may be able to trace its origins to a childhood experience, which can then be reframed or healed through suggestion during hypnosis.

Hypnosis can also be used to modify deeply ingrained habits and behaviors. Because habits are often stored in the subconscious, they are not typically influenced by conscious willpower alone. This is why many people find it difficult to quit smoking, break bad eating habits, or overcome procrastination. Hypnosis works by speaking directly to the subconscious, where these automatic behaviors are rooted. By using specific suggestions or visualizations, a trained hypnotherapist can help individuals replace old, negative behaviors with new, positive ones. For instance, a person who wishes to quit smoking may be guided into a relaxed state and given positive suggestions about their ability to live a smoke-free life, allowing the subconscious mind to accept this new belief and reinforce the desired behavior.

In addition to modifying behaviors, hypnosis is also effective for addressing emotional challenges that are rooted in the subconscious. Conditions like anxiety, depression, and low self-esteem are often influenced by subconscious beliefs and unresolved emotions. Hypnotherapy can help uncover the root causes of these issues and introduce new, healthier ways of thinking and feeling. For example, by accessing and reframing past experiences that may have contributed to feelings of inadequacy or fear, hypnosis can help individuals release emotional blockages and cultivate more positive thought patterns.

One of the most fascinating aspects of accessing the subconscious through hypnosis is its potential to enhance creativity and problem-solving. The relaxed and focused state of hypnosis allows the mind to bypass the usual cognitive filters, making it easier to tap into intuitive insights and creative solutions. Many individuals use hypnosis to overcome mental blocks or enhance their ability to innovate. Whether for artists seeking inspiration or professionals looking for new solutions to complex problems, hypnosis can facilitate access to the subconscious mind's vast creative potential.

The process of accessing the subconscious through hypnosis is safe and non-invasive, provided it is done by a trained and qualified hypnotherapist. Hypnosis is not a form of mind control, and individuals cannot be made to do something against their will or value while under hypnosis. Rather, it is a collaborative process between the therapist and the client, with the client maintaining control over their own experience at all times. The suggestions offered during hypnosis are only effective if they align with the individual's own desires and values, which is why the conscious mind remains an active participant in the process.

In conclusion, hypnosis provides a powerful way to access and influence the subconscious mind. By entering a relaxed and focused state, individuals can bypass the critical filters of the conscious mind and tap into deeper layers of memory, emotion, and behavior. This access allows for the modification of negative habits, the healing of emotional wounds, and the reprogramming of limiting beliefs. Whether used for therapeutic purposes, personal growth, or enhancing creativity, hypnosis offers a unique opportunity to unlock the potential of the subconscious mind and create lasting, positive change.

Power of the Subconscious Mind

The subconscious mind holds immense power, influencing thoughts, behaviors, and emotional responses in ways that often remain hidden from our conscious awareness. Operating beneath the surface of our everyday thinking, the subconscious stores memories, beliefs, and automatic processes that shape our daily lives. It governs many aspects of our actions, including habits, emotional reactions, and even the ways we perceive the world. Hypnosis is a powerful tool for tapping into this vast reservoir of mental resources, allowing individuals to reshape and transform deeply ingrained patterns that may otherwise be difficult to change.

Unlike the conscious mind, which is responsible for active decision-making, reasoning, and immediate awareness, the subconscious operates more automatically. It works in the background, processing information without our conscious effort, and is responsible for controlling basic bodily functions such as heartbeat and breathing. It also houses memories, beliefs, fears, and desires—many of which we may not be fully aware of. This hidden part of the mind plays a crucial role in shaping who we are, influencing how we react to various situations and how we interact with others.

One of the most profound aspects of the subconscious mind is its ability to influence behavior through deeply embedded habits. Habits are formed over time, and once they are established, they are often governed by the subconscious rather than conscious decision-making. For example, when a person reaches for a snack or lights a cigarette in response to stress, these actions have likely become automatic over time, stored in the subconscious as coping mechanisms. Hypnosis allows individuals to access this part of the mind and reprogram these automatic responses, helping them replace unhealthy habits with more constructive behaviors.

Emotional responses are also largely governed by the subconscious. Many of our fears, anxieties, and phobias stem from subconscious beliefs and past experiences, often dating back to childhood. These emotional responses can be triggered by external stimuli without us fully understanding why. Hypnosis can help uncover the root causes of these emotional patterns, enabling individuals to reframe past experiences and release negative emotions. By accessing the subconscious and offering positive suggestions, hypnosis can help individuals break free from emotional patterns that limit their potential, enabling them to respond to challenges with greater calm and resilience.

The power of the subconscious mind is not limited to habits and emotional responses—it also plays a key role in shaping our beliefs and self-concept. The subconscious absorbs messages from our environment, including how we are raised, societal influences, and personal experiences. Over time, these messages become deeply ingrained beliefs about ourselves, others, and the world around us. If these beliefs are negative or limiting, they can influence how we approach life, often without our conscious awareness. Hypnosis can be an effective way to challenge and change these limiting beliefs. Through suggestion and visualization, the subconscious mind can be rewired to adopt more empowering, positive beliefs that can lead to greater self-confidence and success.

Another remarkable aspect of the subconscious is its capacity for creativity. While the conscious mind is often occupied with logic and analysis, the subconscious mind is more fluid and intuitive. Many creative insights, ideas, and solutions emerge from the subconscious, often when the conscious mind is at rest or distracted. This is why people often experience sudden bursts of creativity or problem-solving insights during moments of relaxation, such as during a walk or while drifting off to sleep. Hypnosis can tap into this creative potential by relaxing the conscious mind and allowing the subconscious to come forward, leading to greater inspiration and innovation.

Hypnosis is an effective means of accessing the power of the subconscious. In a relaxed, focused state, the conscious mind steps aside, allowing the subconscious to become more receptive to new suggestions. This is why hypnosis is often used in therapeutic settings to help individuals overcome deep-seated issues such as phobias, addiction, anxiety, and trauma. By working directly with the subconscious, hypnosis can help individuals identify the root causes of their challenges, reframe negative memories, and replace outdated beliefs or behaviors with healthier, more constructive alternatives.

In addition to its therapeutic uses, hypnosis can be used for personal development, performance enhancement, and self-improvement. Athletes, performers, and professionals often use hypnosis to boost confidence, improve focus, and enhance mental clarity. By accessing the subconscious, individuals can tap into the mental resources necessary to achieve peak performance, block out distractions, and visualize success. The subconscious mind can also be used to reinforce positive habits, like healthy eating or regular exercise, helping individuals maintain motivation and consistency.

In conclusion, the subconscious mind is an incredibly powerful force that shapes our thoughts, behaviors, and emotional experiences. It controls many of the automatic processes that govern our lives, including habits, beliefs, and emotional responses. Hypnosis provides a unique opportunity to access and influence the subconscious, offering a pathway to personal transformation and growth. Whether used for overcoming negative behaviors, healing emotional wounds, or enhancing creativity and performance, hypnosis harnesses the immense power of the subconscious mind, enabling individuals to unlock their full potential.

Techniques in Hypnosis

Hypnosis is a therapeutic technique that leverages deep relaxation and focused concentration to access the subconscious mind, facilitating change in thoughts, behaviors, and emotional patterns. Several methods and techniques are employed by trained hypnotists to induce this altered state of consciousness, each designed to work with the mind's natural processes to achieve specific goals, whether for therapeutic healing, self-improvement, or performance enhancement. Understanding these techniques helps illuminate how hypnosis works and how it can be used effectively to bring about meaningful change.

1. Progressive Relaxation Technique

One of the most common and widely used techniques for inducing hypnosis is progressive relaxation. In this method, the individual is guided to progressively relax each muscle group in the body, starting from the toes and working up to the head. The purpose of this technique is to promote deep physical relaxation, which in turn encourages mental relaxation. As the body relaxes, the mind follows, allowing the person to enter a state of heightened focus and receptivity. Progressive relaxation helps ease anxiety, reduce stress, and prepare the mind for deeper work in the subconscious.

2. Eye Fixation Technique

The eye fixation technique involves directing the individual's attention to a particular point or object, often a pendulum, a flickering light, or the hypnotist's finger. The individual is asked to focus all their attention on this object, with the hypnotist providing verbal suggestions to help deepen the state of relaxation. The repetitive nature of focusing on a single point combined with verbal cues helps guide the person's mind into a more suggestible state. This technique is often used in both stage hypnosis and clinical hypnotherapy to induce a trance-like state.

3. Visualization Technique

Visualization is a technique that utilizes the power of mental imagery to facilitate change in the subconscious mind. The individual is guided to imagine vivid and positive scenes, often with the goal of creating a relaxed or empowering mental environment. For example, a person struggling with anxiety might be guided to visualize themselves in a peaceful, serene place, allowing the subconscious to associate relaxation with the mental image. Visualization can also be used to enhance creativity, improve self-confidence, and promote healing by encouraging the mind to picture desired outcomes. The strength of this technique lies in the ability of the mind to respond to detailed and emotional imagery, which can influence subconscious beliefs and behaviors.

4. Direct Suggestion Technique

Direct suggestion is one of the most straightforward and widely used techniques in hypnosis. In this approach, the hypnotist gives clear and specific instructions or suggestions to the subconscious mind. These suggestions may involve changing unwanted behaviors (such as smoking or overeating), alleviating pain, reducing stress, or improving confidence. The key to this method is the hypnotist's ability to communicate in a way that resonates with the subconscious, bypassing the conscious mind's critical filters. Direct suggestion is often used for its simplicity and effectiveness in treating habits, phobias, and stress-related conditions.

5. Indirect Suggestion Technique (Ericksonian Hypnosis)

Indirect suggestion, a technique pioneered by Milton Erickson, is a more subtle and conversational approach to hypnosis. Rather than giving direct commands, the hypnotist uses stories, metaphors, and indirect language to communicate with the subconscious mind. This method is particularly useful for individuals who may be resistant to direct suggestion or for those seeking a more relaxed, conversational experience. The hypnotist may tell a story that mirrors the client's struggles or use symbolic language to help the subconscious mind find solutions. Indirect suggestion is highly effective for dealing with complex issues like trauma or deeply ingrained habits, as it engages the mind's natural problem-solving abilities in a non-threatening way.

6. Anchoring Technique

Anchoring involves associating a particular physical gesture or sensation with a desired emotional state or behavior. The individual is guided into a state of relaxation or confidence, and then a specific action—such as touching the fingers together, tapping the knuckles, or pressing a thumb to the palm—is repeated while in this heightened emotional state. Later, when the person performs the same gesture or action in real life, the subconscious mind is triggered to recreate the emotional state associated with it. Anchoring is often used to help people manage stress, anxiety, or negative emotions by creating an easily accessible "trigger" for relaxation or confidence. This technique is particularly popular in performance enhancement and behavior modification.

7. Age Regression Technique

Age regression is a technique used to guide individuals back to earlier stages of their life, typically childhood, to uncover forgotten memories or emotions that may be influencing their current behaviors or emotional responses. During age regression, the individual is brought into a relaxed state and asked to mentally "revisit" past events, often with the goal of resolving trauma, understanding unresolved emotional conflicts, or reshaping limiting beliefs formed in childhood. This technique is used to address deep-seated issues that stem from earlier experiences and is commonly applied in therapeutic hypnosis to resolve issues like phobias, trauma, or self-esteem problems.

Future Pacing Technique

Future pacing is a technique used to prepare individuals for future events by mentally rehearsing and visualizing successful outcomes. During hypnosis, the client is guided to imagine themselves in a future scenario, such as giving a presentation, handling a stressful situation, or achieving a personal goal. The client mentally rehearses the situation while feeling confident, calm, or empowered. This technique helps the subconscious mind become familiar with the desired outcome and builds a sense of confidence and readiness. It is commonly used to improve performance in areas like public speaking, athletic achievement, or overcoming social anxiety.

Rapid Induction Techniques

Rapid induction techniques are designed to quickly bring an individual into a hypnotic state, often in just a few minutes. These methods are often used in situations where time is limited, or in stage hypnosis settings where the goal is to induce hypnosis on multiple people quickly. Examples of rapid induction techniques include the handshake induction, where the hypnotist abruptly shakes the person's hand and uses a verbal cue to trigger relaxation, or the rapid countdown method, where the individual is instructed to relax progressively with each count. While these methods are quick, they still rely on the same principles of focus, relaxation, and suggestion that are foundational to hypnosis.

Conclusion

The diverse techniques used in hypnosis allow it to be applied to a variety of therapeutic and personal development goals. From overcoming habits and releasing emotional blockages to enhancing creativity and performance, these methods offer flexible and effective tools for accessing the subconscious mind. By utilizing different approaches, such as progressive relaxation, visualization, direct suggestion, or age regression, hypnosis can be tailored to meet the unique needs of the individual, helping them achieve lasting change and personal growth.

Inducing a Hypnotic Trance

Inducing a hypnotic trance involves guiding an individual into a state of focused attention and deep relaxation, where the conscious mind becomes less active, and the subconscious becomes more receptive to suggestions. This process is not about controlling the individual's mind, but rather about helping them access a heightened state of awareness where they are more open to positive changes, emotional healing, and behavior modification. The technique relies on various methods to help the person enter this altered state of consciousness, where the usual mental filters are temporarily bypassed, allowing for deeper communication with the subconscious mind.

The first step in inducing a hypnotic trance is creating a calm and comfortable environment. The individual is typically asked to sit or lie down in a quiet space, free from distractions. Soft lighting, soothing music, or gentle sounds may be used to enhance the atmosphere, helping the person relax further. It is crucial that the individual feels safe and at ease, as this fosters a sense of trust and comfort, which is essential for successful hypnosis.

Progressive Relaxation

One of the most common techniques used to induce a hypnotic trance is progressive relaxation. This method involves guiding the individual to progressively relax each part of their body, from their toes to their head. As each muscle group is relaxed, the person is encouraged to focus on the sensation of releasing tension and letting go of any stress or discomfort. By the time the person reaches the head and neck, they should feel deeply relaxed and centered. Progressive relaxation not only calms the body but also helps quiet the mind, setting the stage for deeper states of hypnosis.

Focused Attention

Once the body is relaxed, the next step is to narrow the individual's focus of attention. This can be achieved by having them concentrate on a specific point, object, or even their breath. One common method is the "eye fixation technique," where the person is asked to focus on an object or the hypnotist's hand. As their attention is drawn to a single point, they naturally begin to tune out other stimuli, helping to enter a state of deep concentration. The more narrowly the individual focuses, the easier it becomes to guide them into a hypnotic trance.

Breathing Techniques

Breathing plays a crucial role in the induction process. Slow, deep breaths encourage relaxation and signal to the body that it is time to shift into a more relaxed state. By encouraging steady, rhythmic breathing, the hypnotist can help calm the nervous system and deepen the sense of tranquility. As the person breathes deeply, they are also encouraged to visualize the air flowing in and out of their body, further enhancing their focus and concentration.

Countdown and Deepening Techniques

Another popular method for inducing a trance is the use of countdowns. The hypnotist may ask the individual to imagine themselves descending a staircase or counting down from ten to one, with each number representing a deeper state of relaxation. As the countdown progresses, the hypnotist may suggest that the individual feels more and more relaxed, allowing them to let go of any remaining tension or distractions. This deepening technique helps deepen the trance, taking the individual into a more profound state of hypnosis.

Visualization

Visualization is a powerful tool for inducing a hypnotic trance. By encouraging the individual to imagine a calming, serene environment, such as a peaceful beach or a tranquil forest, the mind can be guided to enter a more relaxed and suggestible state. In these visualizations, the person may be asked to vividly imagine details like the sights, sounds, and smells of the scene. This immersive experience helps focus the mind, pushing aside any intrusive thoughts or distractions, and making the person more open to hypnotic suggestions.

Receptivity to Suggestion

As the individual enters a deeper trance, the conscious mind becomes more passive, and the subconscious mind becomes more active. This makes the individual more receptive to positive suggestions. Hypnotists will often use this phase to introduce therapeutic suggestions—such as promoting relaxation, confidence, or the cessation of unhealthy habits. These suggestions can be directly related to the individual's goals, like reducing stress, eliminating a fear, or overcoming an addiction. The deeper the trance, the more effectively the subconscious mind can absorb and accept these suggestions.

The Role of Trust and Relaxation

A critical element in inducing a hypnotic trance is the establishment of trust between the hypnotist and the individual. The person must feel safe, respected, and comfortable with the process for the trance to be effective. If a person is anxious or distrustful, they are unlikely to enter a deep state of hypnosis. That's why establishing rapport and ensuring the person feels in control are essential for success. Hypnosis is not a form of manipulation; rather, it is a collaborative process between the individual and the hypnotist, with the individual always maintaining the ability to "wake up" or end the session at any time.

The State of Hypnosis

When the individual reaches a hypnotic trance, they may experience a sense of deep relaxation, a detachment from the surrounding environment, or a heightened awareness of their internal state. Contrary to popular belief, individuals in a trance are not asleep or unconscious. Instead, they are in an altered state of focused concentration, where they may be more aware of their thoughts and feelings than in their usual waking state. In this state, individuals can explore deeper layers of the mind, release emotional blockages, and make lasting changes, whether through therapeutic techniques or performance enhancement.

Conclusion

Inducing a hypnotic trance involves several key steps: creating a relaxing environment, using techniques to relax the body and focus the mind, and employing visualization and suggestion to deepen the trance. Through methods like progressive relaxation, eye fixation, and deep breathing, the individual's mind becomes more open and receptive, allowing for meaningful therapeutic change. As hypnosis works by facilitating a connection between the conscious and subconscious minds, the process of entering a trance is a powerful tool for transformation, healing, and personal growth.

Deepening Techniques

Once an individual has entered a relaxed state during hypnosis, deepening techniques are used to take them further into a heightened state of concentration and suggestibility. These techniques are essential for facilitating deeper levels of relaxation, allowing the hypnotist to guide the person into a more profound trance where the subconscious mind becomes even more accessible. The deeper the trance, the more effective the hypnosis can be for therapeutic change, such as overcoming phobias, managing pain, or altering unwanted behaviors.

1. Countdown Method

One of the most commonly used deepening techniques is the countdown method. This technique typically involves having the individual imagine descending a staircase or counting backward from a specific number, such as 10 to 1. With each step or number, the individual is encouraged to relax further, sinking deeper into a state of calm and receptivity. The hypnotist may suggest that with each count, they feel more relaxed and more deeply focused, allowing them to "let go" and drift deeper into trance. This gradual descent helps ease the person into a more profound state of hypnosis.

2. Fractionation

Fractionation is a technique that involves bringing the individual in and out of a light trance, then deepening it again. The idea behind fractionation is that by allowing the person to experience states of relaxation and alertness repeatedly, they learn to enter deep hypnosis more quickly and easily. After the person is brought back into a more relaxed state following a brief period of alertness, they often experience a deeper level of trance than before. This technique can be very effective for reinforcing the hypnotic state, helping the individual quickly return to a deeper state whenever they choose to do so.

3. Deepening with Imagery and Sensory Focus

Imagery is another powerful tool for deepening hypnosis. In this technique, the individual is guided to imagine themselves in a peaceful, serene setting, such as walking through a forest, floating on a cloud, or descending into a tranquil cave. As the individual immerses themselves in the sensory details of the environment—hearing the sounds of nature, feeling the warmth of the sun, or noticing the colors and textures around them—they become more absorbed in the experience, which deepens the trance. The hypnotist may encourage the individual to focus on specific sensations (such as the feeling of warmth or the sound of a gentle breeze) to further amplify the relaxation and focus.

4. The Elevator Technique

The elevator technique is similar to the countdown method, but it uses the metaphor of an elevator to guide the individual deeper into hypnosis. The person is asked to imagine themselves stepping into an elevator, which is then taken down to a lower floor. With each floor the elevator descends, the individual feels more relaxed and deeply focused. The hypnotist may suggest that with each descent, the person moves closer to a more profound and receptive state of mind. This method can also be paired with other suggestions, such as feeling more deeply relaxed with each floor or experiencing greater calmness as the elevator moves downward.

5. Rapid Deepening Techniques

Some hypnotists use rapid deepening techniques, which are designed to bring the individual into a deeper state of trance quickly. One example is the "snap induction," where the hypnotist may snap their fingers or make a sharp sound to signal the person to sink deeper into hypnosis. This sudden shift in focus, combined with verbal suggestions, can quickly deepen the trance. Another example is the "hand drop" technique, where the hypnotist asks the individual to raise their hand and then drop it while suggesting that the hand will become very heavy, pulling them deeper into relaxation. These techniques rely on the power of suggestion and the element of surprise to deepen the individual's focus and relaxation.

6. Progressive Relaxation Deepening

After the initial relaxation, the hypnotist may use progressive relaxation techniques to further deepen the state. This can involve asking the individual to mentally scan their body, starting from the head and moving downward, consciously relaxing each body part. The hypnotist might suggest that with every exhale, the person releases more tension, and with every breath, they feel even more relaxed and calm. Progressive relaxation not only helps to deepen the hypnotic state but also reinforces the connection between the mind and body, making it easier for the individual to enter trance during future sessions.

7. Anchoring Deepening

Anchoring is a technique that involves associating a physical sensation or gesture with a deepened state of relaxation. For example, the hypnotist may suggest that the individual press their thumb and forefinger together, and each time they do so, they will feel a wave of relaxation. The subconscious mind learns to associate the gesture with the relaxed state, and by repeating the gesture in the future, the person can quickly return to that state f calm. Anchoring can be used during the deepening phase to reinforce the feeling of relaxation and to help individuals deepen the trance state with physical cues.

. Breathwork and Pausing

Controlled breathwork, combined with strategic pauses, is a subtle but effective way to deepen hypnosis. The hypnotist might guide the individual to take deep, slow breaths, with each breath allowing them to relax further. Pausing between suggestions also helps. These pauses allow the person to absorb and internalize the suggestions, deepening the trance in the process. The rhythm of breathing and pauses creates a calming effect, which encourages the individual to sink deeper into the hypnotic state.

. Deepening with Voice and Language

The hypnotist's tone of voice and use of language also play an important role in deepening the trance. A soft, soothing tone, combined with slow, deliberate speech, can guide the individual deeper into hypnosis. Verbal cues like "deeper and deeper," "relax more with each breath," or "with every word I say, you feel yourself going deeper" can reinforce the experience. The hypnotist may also use language that emphasizes deepening sensations, such as suggesting that the person's body feels heavier, more relaxed, or more focused as they continue to relax.

Conclusion

Deepening techniques are an essential part of the hypnotic process, helping individuals achieve a deeper state of relaxation and heightened suggestibility. By using methods like countdowns, visualization, and anchoring, a hypnotist can guide someone into a profound trance where therapeutic work, behavior modification, and emotional healing can occur. These techniques work by reinforcing relaxation, enhancing focus, and allowing the subconscious mind to become more receptive to positive change, making them a valuable tool for both hypnotherapists and those seeking to explore the potential of hypnosis.

Suggestions Techniques

In hypnosis, suggestion techniques are at the core of the process, as they are used to guid
the subconscious mind toward desired changes in behavior, thought patterns, or
emotional responses. Once an individual has reached a relaxed, focused state, their
subconscious becomes more receptive to suggestions, making it an ideal time to
introduce positive, constructive changes. The effectiveness of these techniques depends
on how well the hypnotist can communicate with the subconscious mind, bypassing the
critical filters of the conscious mind.

1. Direct Suggestion

Direct suggestion is one of the most straightforward and commonly used techniques in
hypnosis. It involves giving clear, simple, and unambiguous instructions to the
subconscious mind. For example, a person trying to quit smoking might be given the
direct suggestion, "You no longer crave cigarettes, and you feel healthy and strong
without them." This method works best when the individual is highly receptive and ready
for change. The key to successful direct suggestion is ensuring that the language used
resonates with the person's desires and values, making it more likely that the
subconscious mind will accept and act upon the suggestion.

2. Indirect Suggestion (Ericksonian Hypnosis)

Indirect suggestion is a more subtle approach, developed by Milton Erickson, which
involves using stories, metaphors, or casual conversation to communicate with the
subconscious mind. Instead of issuing a direct command, the hypnotist might say
something like, "Some people find that when they focus on their breathing, they can feel
more relaxed," or "It's interesting how some people are able to easily make changes whe
they're ready." This technique allows the subconscious to interpret the suggestion in a
way that feels less like a command and more like a natural, personal discovery. Indirect
suggestion is especially useful for individuals who may be resistant to more direct
methods or those dealing with complex issues, as it engages the mind in a less
confrontational manner.

3. Post-Hypnotic Suggestion

Post-hypnotic suggestion involves giving the individual instructions or suggestions that
will take effect after the hypnosis session has ended. For example, the hypnotist might

suggest, "After you wake up from this session, every time you take a deep breath, you'll feel more calm and confident." The power of post-hypnotic suggestion lies in its ability to influence future behavior or emotional responses. By embedding these suggestions into the subconscious during the hypnotic state, they can have a lasting impact, often resulting in immediate or gradual change once the person returns to their normal state of awareness.

4. Visualization Suggestions

Visualization is a potent technique for creating vivid mental images that help the subconscious mind understand and internalize desired changes. In this method, the hypnotist may guide the individual to vividly imagine a scene or experience related to the desired outcome. For example, a person trying to overcome a fear of flying might be asked to imagine themselves in a plane, feeling completely calm and relaxed as they soar through the skies. The imagery used in these suggestions should be detailed and sensory-rich, involving sights, sounds, smells, and feelings, making the experience feel real and emotionally engaging. Visualization helps the subconscious mind associate positive experiences with specific situations, making it more likely that the person will act in alignment with the desired change in the future.

5. Future Pacing

Future pacing is a suggestion technique where the hypnotist helps the individual mentally rehearse and visualize themselves achieving their goals or successfully handling future situations. This method encourages the subconscious to "practice" desired behaviors and emotional responses before they are actually needed. For instance, if someone is trying to manage stress, the hypnotist might suggest, "Imagine yourself in a stressful situation, and see yourself handling it with ease and calmness. You're in control, and you remain relaxed and confident." By mentally preparing the individual for future scenarios, future pacing helps reinforce the idea that success is not only possible but already being prepared for in the subconscious mind.

6. Affirmations and Positive Suggestions

Affirmations are positive statements that reinforce the individual's desired beliefs or behaviors. These statements are often repeated during hypnosis to embed them deeply in the subconscious. Examples include, "I am confident," "I am calm in every situation," or "I am in control of my habits." These affirmations are powerful because they counteract negative self-talk or limiting beliefs by replacing them with positive, empowering thoughts. During hypnosis, the repetition of these affirmations allows them to bypass the conscious mind's usual filters, directly influencing the subconscious to accept them as truth.

7. Confusion Technique

The confusion technique is a more advanced and creative suggestion method, often associated with Ericksonian hypnosis. It involves creating a mild state of confusion or uncertainty in the conscious mind, which makes it easier for the subconscious to accept new suggestions. For example, a hypnotist might ask a person to focus on several contradictory ideas or instructions at once. As the conscious mind struggles to process the conflicting information, the subconscious becomes more open to suggestions. This technique is effective because it temporarily overloads the conscious mind, which then allows the subconscious to absorb suggestions more easily.

8. Reframing

Reframing is a technique where the hypnotist helps the individual reinterpret or view an experience, belief, or situation from a different perspective. This can be especially powerful for individuals who are dealing with negative thought patterns or traumatic experiences. For example, if someone has a fear of public speaking, the hypnotist might suggest, "Instead of feeling nervous about speaking, you can view it as an exciting opportunity to share your ideas with others." Reframing shifts the emotional response to an event, helping the subconscious mind to associate it with more positive, empowering feelings.

9. Anchoring

Anchoring involves associating a specific physical gesture, sensation, or mental image with a positive state of mind or behavior. During hypnosis, the individual is encouraged to recall a moment when they felt confident, calm, or empowered, and a specific "anchor" is created—such as touching two fingers together or visualizing a particular image. The hypnotist then suggests that whenever the individual uses this anchor, they will automatically return to that positive state. Anchoring works by creating a mental link between the physical action or image and the emotional or mental state, allowing the individual to access the positive state at will.

10. The Conversational Method

The conversational method, often used in covert hypnosis, involves weaving suggestions into a natural conversation. Rather than using formal induction techniques, the hypnotist speaks in a calm, persuasive tone, subtly embedding suggestions within the conversation. This technique takes advantage of natural, everyday speech patterns, often making the person unaware of the suggestions being made. It can be particularly useful in situations where direct hypnosis is not appropriate, such as during therapy sessions or in casual settings. The subconscious mind is constantly processing information, and the conversational method helps plant seeds of change in a non-intrusive way.

Conclusion

Suggestion techniques are the foundation of hypnosis, providing a powerful way to influence the subconscious mind and create lasting changes. By using methods such as direct suggestion, visualization, future pacing, and reframing, the hypnotist can help individuals overcome challenges, modify behaviors, and achieve their goals. Whether the suggestions are subtle or direct, the success of these techniques depends on the individual's receptivity, the quality of the language used, and the depth of the hypnotic trance. These methods are not only therapeutic but can also be applied for personal growth, performance enhancement, and emotional well-being.

Hypnosis for Stress Management

Hypnosis has become an increasingly popular tool for managing stress, offering a natural, effective way to reduce anxiety and promote relaxation. When someone is under stress, their body releases stress hormones like cortisol and adrenaline, triggering the "fight or flight" response. This physiological reaction can lead to heightened feelings of anxiety, physical tension, and mental exhaustion. Hypnosis addresses stress by helping individuals access a deeply relaxed state, allowing the body and mind to release tension, regulate emotions, and reset the stress response.

The process of hypnosis involves guiding the individual into a state of deep relaxation and focused attention. In this state, the conscious mind becomes less active, while the subconscious becomes more open to positive suggestions. These suggestions can help the person change their response to stress, reducing feelings of anxiety and promoting a sense of calm and control.

1. Deep Relaxation and Stress Reduction

One of the most immediate benefits of hypnosis for stress management is its ability to induce profound relaxation. During a typical session, a trained hypnotherapist may guide the individual through a series of relaxation exercises, such as progressive muscle relaxation or guided imagery. These techniques help reduce the physical symptoms of stress, such as muscle tension, rapid breathing, and elevated heart rate. As the person becomes more relaxed, their body begins to shift out of the "fight or flight" response and into the "rest and digest" mode, where stress hormones decrease and the body can begin to heal and restore balance.

2. Addressing the Root Causes of Stress

Hypnosis is not just about alleviating the immediate symptoms of stress; it can also help individuals identify and address the root causes of their stress. Through techniques such as regression or exploring subconscious beliefs, hypnosis can uncover hidden triggers— whether they are related to past trauma, unresolved emotional issues, or limiting thought patterns—that contribute to the person's current stress. Once these underlying causes are brought to light, the individual can work through them with the help of the hypnotherapist, allowing for deeper emotional healing and long-term stress reduction.

3. Reprogramming the Mind's Stress Response

hrough hypnosis, individuals can reprogram their subconscious mind to respond to tress in a healthier way. In a relaxed state, the hypnotherapist may suggest new ways of hinking about or reacting to stressful situations. For example, instead of viewing a hallenging work deadline as an overwhelming threat, the person might be encouraged to iew it as an exciting challenge that can be tackled one step at a time. Over time, these ositive suggestions become ingrained in the subconscious mind, which helps the ndividual develop a more resilient and adaptive approach to stress.

. Reducing Anxiety and Panic Attacks

Chronic stress often leads to anxiety, and in some cases, it can trigger panic attacks. Iypnosis has been shown to be effective in reducing the frequency and intensity of nxiety and panic episodes. During hypnosis, individuals are guided to access a calm, entered state, where they can mentally rehearse calming techniques or visualize hemselves handling anxiety-provoking situations with ease. Suggestions may include eep breathing, relaxation, and the visualization of a peaceful, safe space. By practicing hese strategies in a deeply relaxed state, the person becomes more equipped to manage heir anxiety in real-life situations.

. Mindfulness and Stress Awareness

Iypnosis can also enhance mindfulness—the ability to stay present and aware of the urrent moment without judgment. Many stressors are caused by overthinking, worrying bout the future, or dwelling on past events. Through hypnosis, individuals can develop he skill of mindfulness, allowing them to focus on the present moment and release the nental clutter that contributes to stress. This shift in awareness can help them approach tressful situations with greater clarity, calmness, and emotional balance.

. Building Coping Strategies

Iypnosis is not only about reducing stress in the moment; it also helps individuals levelop long-term coping strategies. A hypnotherapist can work with the person to trengthen their ability to manage stress when it arises, whether through developing ealthier thought patterns or creating mental "anchors" for relaxation. For instance, the ypnotherapist might teach the individual how to use deep breathing techniques or mental magery to regain a sense of calm whenever they feel stress building. These tools mpower the person to take control of their stress response and apply the techniques in heir everyday life.

. Enhancing Sleep and Relaxation

Stress is often linked to poor sleep, as anxiety can keep individuals awake at night, reventing restful sleep. Hypnosis can improve sleep quality by addressing the mental and physical tension that contributes to insomnia. Suggestions can be made to promote a sense of peace and tranquility before bedtime, making it easier for the individual to fall asleep and stay asleep. Additionally, hypnosis can help break the cycle of stress-induced insomnia by teaching the subconscious mind to associate sleep with relaxation rather than anxiety or worry.

8. Self-Hypnosis for Stress Management

One of the most empowering aspects of hypnosis for stress management is the ability to practice self-hypnosis. After working with a hypnotherapist, many individuals learn how to enter a relaxed state on their own, using techniques such as focused breathing or visualization. Self-hypnosis provides a convenient and effective tool for managing stress in real-time, whether at home, at work, or in stressful social situations. By regularly practicing self-hypnosis, individuals can strengthen their ability to manage stress independently and improve their overall resilience.

9. Pain Management and Stress Relief

Stress can exacerbate physical pain, creating a cycle where discomfort leads to more stress, and stress increases sensitivity to pain. Hypnosis can be effective in breaking this cycle by helping individuals manage both their stress and pain simultaneously. By suggesting relaxation, reducing tension, and promoting healing imagery, hypnosis can lower pain perception and reduce the emotional toll that pain can take on an individual. This makes hypnosis a valuable tool for those experiencing chronic pain, as it addresses the stress-related components of their discomfort.

10. Long-Term Benefits

While hypnosis can provide immediate relief from stress, its benefits extend beyond the hypnosis session itself. Regular sessions can lead to lasting changes in the way the person responds to stress, improving overall well-being and mental health. Many individuals report a long-term reduction in stress levels, increased feelings of calm and control, and a more positive outlook on life. Over time, hypnosis helps individuals develop a deeper understanding of their stress triggers and a greater sense of mastery over their emotional responses.

Conclusion

Hypnosis offers a highly effective and holistic approach to managing stress, providing individuals with the tools to reduce anxiety, reprogram their responses to stress, and enhance their overall well-being. By addressing both the physical and psychological components of stress, hypnosis promotes a deep sense of relaxation and emotional balance. Whether through direct suggestions, visualization, or self-hypnosis, hypnosis helps individuals manage stress in the short term and build long-term resilience, making it a valuable tool for improving mental and emotional health.

Hypnosis and Relaxation

Hypnosis is often associated with relaxation due to its ability to induce a deep sense of calm and tranquility. At its core, hypnosis is a state of focused attention and heightened suggestibility, which allows the mind and body to enter a deeply relaxed state. This relaxation is not only beneficial for reducing stress, but it can also promote physical and mental well-being by encouraging a sense of peace, helping to relieve tension, and improving overall health.

The process of hypnosis typically begins with relaxation techniques designed to ease the individual into a trance-like state. This state is characterized by reduced brain activity, slower heart rate, and a deep sense of calm. As the person becomes more relaxed, the conscious mind quiets, allowing the subconscious mind to become more receptive to positive suggestions and therapeutic interventions.

1. Inducing Deep Relaxation

One of the primary goals of hypnosis is to help individuals achieve deep relaxation, which involves both the body and the mind. In a typical session, the hypnotist will guide the person through progressive relaxation exercises, where they are encouraged to focus on each muscle group, consciously relaxing them one by one. As muscle tension dissipates, the individual's physical state becomes more relaxed, and this can help to reduce feelings of stress and anxiety.

Deep relaxation also triggers the body's parasympathetic nervous system, the "rest and digest" system, which counters the "fight or flight" response that is activated by stress. This shift helps to lower heart rate, blood pressure, and levels of the stress hormone cortisol, promoting an overall sense of calm and well-being.

2. Enhanced Sensory Focus

In a relaxed state, the individual's awareness of their environment becomes narrowed, which helps them focus more deeply on the present moment. This heightened sensory focus is a key element of hypnosis. The hypnotist may guide the individual to imagine a peaceful scene, such as a beach, forest, or garden, and ask them to immerse themselves in the sensory details of the environment. By concentrating on the sounds of the waves, the smell of the trees, or the sensation of the breeze, the individual's mind becomes deeply absorbed, and stress and distractions begin to fade away. This immersive experience creates a sense of calm and contentment, contributing to overall relaxation.

3. Relaxation Through Breathwork

Breathing is a powerful tool in hypnosis for relaxation. A common technique is to guide the person to take slow, deep breaths, focusing on inhaling through the nose, holding briefly, and then exhaling through the mouth. Deep breathing activates the body's relaxation response by increasing oxygen flow, calming the nervous system, and helping to release physical tension. By incorporating focused breathing into the hypnotic process, individuals can quickly enter a relaxed state and maintain a sense of calm throughout the session.

4. Reducing Physical Tension

Hypnosis also helps to alleviate physical tension, which is often a symptom of stress and anxiety. The body's muscles naturally tense up in response to emotional strain, leading to discomfort and even pain. During hypnosis, the individual is encouraged to mentally scan their body, noticing areas of tightness or discomfort and then focusing on releasing that tension. This practice, combined with deep relaxation techniques, can reduce symptoms like headaches, muscle soreness, and even chronic pain. Many people who use hypnosis regularly for relaxation report feeling more physically comfortable and experiencing fewer stress-related symptoms.

5. Enhanced Mental Relaxation

In addition to its physical benefits, hypnosis helps to achieve mental relaxation by quieting the conscious mind. In our daily lives, the conscious mind is often consumed with worries, to-do lists, and mental chatter, making it difficult to experience peace. During hypnosis, the conscious mind becomes less active, and the individual enters a more focused and receptive state. The hypnotist may suggest positive thoughts or peaceful imagery, which helps to displace negative or anxious thoughts and encourages a more tranquil mental state.

This mental relaxation is not only beneficial for reducing stress, but it also allows the individual to access deeper emotional and psychological layers. It provides an opportunity for healing, self-reflection, and personal growth, as the mind is freed from distractions and is better able to process emotions and thoughts in a relaxed manner.

6. Relaxation as a Foundation for Therapeutic Change

The relaxation induced by hypnosis is not just about temporary stress relief—it also forms the foundation for long-term therapeutic change. Once the individual is in a deeply relaxed state, they become more receptive to positive suggestions, which can help address various issues such as anxiety, insomnia, smoking cessation, or chronic pain. For example, someone struggling with sleep issues may be given suggestions to associate sleep with deep relaxation, creating a positive mental framework that encourages restful sleep even outside of hypnosis sessions.

Similarly, relaxation techniques can be used to help individuals overcome stress-related behaviors. By deeply relaxing the mind and body and introducing new thought patterns, hypnosis helps reprogram the subconscious to adopt healthier responses to stress, making it easier to cope with challenges in everyday life.

7. Self-Hypnosis for Relaxation

Another key benefit of hypnosis for relaxation is the ability to practice self-hypnosis. Self-hypnosis involves using the techniques learned in a professional session to enter a state of relaxation on your own. This can be especially helpful for people who need to manage stress or anxiety on a day-to-day basis. Individuals can use self-hypnosis techniques, such as focused breathing, visualization, or progressive muscle relaxation, to create their own peaceful mental space whenever they feel tension building. Over time, the ability to self-hypnotize becomes a valuable tool for maintaining relaxation and managing stress outside of therapy sessions.

8. Relaxation and Emotional Well-being

The deep relaxation achieved through hypnosis not only helps to manage physical symptoms of stress but also contributes to emotional well-being. When an individual is relaxed, they are more able to access their inner resources, whether it's a sense of calm, self-compassion, or confidence. By creating a relaxed mental and emotional space, hypnosis encourages the person to feel more at peace with themselves and the world around them. This emotional equilibrium helps to buffer against the impact of future stressors, making it easier to maintain a balanced, positive outlook on life.

Conclusion

Hypnosis is a highly effective tool for inducing relaxation, offering both immediate relief from stress and long-term benefits for mental and physical health. By guiding the individual into a deeply relaxed state, hypnosis promotes relaxation through techniques like deep breathing, sensory focus, and progressive muscle relaxation. These techniques not only help reduce stress but also facilitate therapeutic change by reprogramming the subconscious mind to respond to stress more effectively. Whether through professional sessions or self-hypnosis practices, hypnosis can significantly improve relaxation, emotional well-being, and overall quality of life.

Stress and the Subconscious Mind

tress is not just a mental or emotional experience; it also has deep physiological roots, ften embedded within the subconscious mind. While the conscious mind processes nmediate, external triggers like deadlines or interpersonal conflicts, the subconscious olds onto the long-term effects of these stresses, influencing how we react and how our odies respond. This deeper layer of the mind can either exacerbate or alleviate stress, epending on how it processes and stores stressful experiences.

Vhen we face stress, our conscious mind quickly identifies threats and responds by ctivating the "fight or flight" system—raising heart rates, increasing blood pressure, and iggering an emotional reaction. However, it's the subconscious mind that often retains ie emotional residue of these experiences, which can perpetuate feelings of anxiety, ension, or unease long after the stressful event has passed. For example, a person who as experienced trauma or prolonged stress might subconsciously react with anxiety even 1 situations where there is no immediate threat, simply because their subconscious mind ssociates similar circumstances with past stressors.

. Subconscious Memory and Stress

he subconscious mind is a vast storehouse of memories, beliefs, and emotional esponses. Experiences of stress, especially those from childhood or formative years, can ecome deeply embedded within this mental space. When faced with similar stressors ater in life, the subconscious mind may trigger automatic responses based on past xperiences. For instance, someone who has been frequently criticized may ubconsciously feel stressed or defensive when receiving feedback, even if the criticism s constructive and not threatening.

hese ingrained responses are often automatic, meaning the individual may not even be onsciously aware of why they're feeling stressed in certain situations. The subconscious nind, however, operates as an emotional recorder, storing patterns of thought, behavior, nd emotional reactions to stressful situations. This is why, even in the absence of new xternal threats, stress-related feelings can persist and resurface, creating a cycle of nxiety and tension.

. Stress and Unresolved Emotional Blocks

Jnresolved emotional experiences can be a significant source of subconscious stress. Past raumas, whether physical, emotional, or psychological, can leave emotional imprints that continue to influence how an individual reacts to stress later in life. These unresolved emotions may manifest as chronic stress, even if the person is unaware of the root cause. For example, someone who has experienced a traumatic event might harbor subconscious feelings of fear or insecurity, which can surface as stress when they encounter similar circumstances or even unrelated stressors.

In these cases, hypnosis can be a useful tool for accessing the subconscious and identifying the emotional blocks that contribute to ongoing stress. Through deep relaxation, the individual can be guided to confront and release stored emotions, which can lead to a reduction in stress and an overall sense of emotional healing. By accessing the subconscious, hypnosis can help the individual work through unresolved emotions and reframe their responses to past experiences, reducing the hold these experiences have on their current stress levels.

3. Beliefs and Thought Patterns Behind Stress

The subconscious mind also holds the beliefs and thought patterns that influence how we perceive and react to stress. If someone believes, at a subconscious level, that they are incapable of handling challenges or that the world is unsafe, they are more likely to perceive neutral or minor events as major sources of stress. These limiting beliefs shape the body's stress response, making it more difficult for the individual to manage anxiety or frustration.

Hypnosis can help by identifying these subconscious beliefs and replacing them with more constructive, empowering ones. For instance, a person who believes they are constantly under pressure might be led to reframe their thinking, accepting that some stress is manageable and that they are capable of dealing with challenges in a calm and composed manner. Through repeated suggestions and mental reframing during hypnosis, individuals can shift their subconscious beliefs about stress, allowing them to approach situations with a healthier, more balanced mindset.

4. The Role of the Subconscious in Chronic Stress

Chronic stress often occurs when the subconscious mind continues to respond to perceived threats or anxieties even when the stressor is no longer present. The body's "fight or flight" response can become triggered repeatedly, leading to long-term physical symptoms such as tension, headaches, digestive issues, and even cardiovascular problems. This ongoing state of stress can create a feedback loop, where the subconscious mind continuously reinforces the stress response, further exacerbating the individual's stress levels.

Hypnosis can break this cycle by reprogramming the subconscious to respond differently to stress. In a relaxed, hypnotic state, suggestions can be given to the subconscious to release stored tension, reduce anxiety, and alter the automatic stress response. Over time, with repeated sessions, the subconscious can begin to respond more appropriately to stress, reducing its frequency and intensity.

5. Stress Reduction Through Hypnotic Suggestions

Once an individual is in a relaxed, hypnotic state, the subconscious becomes more receptive to suggestions for stress reduction. Hypnotherapists use techniques such as guided imagery, progressive muscle relaxation, and positive affirmations to help the person reframe their experience of stress. For instance, they may suggest that the individual can choose to respond to stress in a calm and controlled manner, or visualize a peaceful, stress-free environment to counteract feelings of anxiety.

Because the subconscious mind is more open during hypnosis, these suggestions can have a powerful and lasting effect, shifting the individual's perception of stress and reducing the emotional and physical impact it has on their daily life. Hypnotic suggestions can also help to create new, healthier habits and coping strategies that the person can use in the face of stress, empowering them to handle difficult situations with greater ease and resilience.

6. The Subconscious and the Relaxation Response

The subconscious mind is not only responsible for storing stress-related memories and beliefs but also plays a key role in activating the body's relaxation response. During hypnosis, the mind can be guided to access a state of deep relaxation, in which the body's natural healing mechanisms are activated. This relaxation response helps to lower blood pressure, reduce heart rate, and decrease levels of stress hormones, all of which counteract the physical effects of stress.

By engaging the subconscious mind in relaxation, hypnosis allows the body to reset its stress response, promoting a sense of calm and well-being. With repeated hypnosis sessions, individuals can learn to enter a relaxed state more easily, even outside of therapy, allowing them to manage stress more effectively in their daily lives.

7. Long-Term Benefits of Hypnosis for Stress

The long-term benefits of using hypnosis to address subconscious stress are significant. As hypnosis helps to identify and reprogram stress-inducing beliefs, release stored emotional blocks, and promote relaxation, it can result in lasting changes in how the subconscious processes stress. Many individuals who use hypnosis for stress management report feeling more resilient, focused, and in control of their emotional responses. Over time, the subconscious mind can develop new, healthier patterns that make stress more manageable and less intrusive in daily life.

Conclusion

Stress, while often a natural and temporary response to external pressures, can become a deeply ingrained issue when stored in the subconscious mind. By accessing and addressing the subconscious, hypnosis provides a powerful method for reducing stress, releasing emotional blocks, and changing harmful thought patterns. Whether through identifying underlying causes, reframing beliefs, or promoting relaxation, hypnosis can help individuals break free from chronic stress, leading to improved emotional health, better physical well-being, and greater overall life satisfaction.

Post-Hypnotic Suggestions for Stress Relief

Post-hypnotic suggestions are a powerful tool used in hypnosis to create lasting changes in behavior and thought patterns, especially when it comes to stress relief. These suggestions are given while the person is in a deeply relaxed, hypnotic state, and they are designed to influence how the individual responds to stress once they have come out of the trance. Unlike suggestions that work only during the hypnotic session, post-hypnotic suggestions remain with the individual after the session is over, gradually shaping their responses and behaviors in daily life.

The effectiveness of post-hypnotic suggestions lies in the ability of the subconscious mind to absorb and store these positive suggestions, making them accessible when the person encounters stressful situations later on. These suggestions can range from simple affirmations to specific instructions on how to handle stress, and their purpose is to help the person manage anxiety, promote relaxation, and foster a more balanced response to life's pressures.

1. Mechanism of Post-Hypnotic Suggestions

During hypnosis, the conscious mind is relaxed and the subconscious becomes more receptive to suggestion. This state of heightened suggestibility allows the therapist to introduce post-hypnotic suggestions that the individual's subconscious mind will carry with them after the session. For instance, a hypnotist might suggest that the individual will feel calm and relaxed whenever they take a deep breath or that they will automatically feel more in control and peaceful when they encounter a stressful situation.

Once these suggestions are introduced, the subconscious mind begins to accept them as part of the individual's internal programming. This can lead to automatic, subconscious responses that are designed to reduce stress, even in situations where the individual might have previously felt anxious or overwhelmed.

2. Types of Post-Hypnotic Suggestions for Stress Relief

There are several different types of post-hypnotic suggestions that can be used to help individuals manage stress:

- **Relaxation Triggers:** A common post-hypnotic suggestion is to provide the individual with a relaxation trigger—something they can do or think about when they need to reduce stress. This might include suggestions like "Whenever you take three deep breaths, you will feel calm and at peace." These triggers work by creating an association between a simple action (like breathing deeply) and a calm, relaxed state, which the subconscious mind learns to replicate in stressful situations.
- **Automatic Stress Management:** Another effective post-hypnotic suggestion is to instruct the subconscious mind to automatically manage stress in specific situations. For example, a hypnotist might suggest, "Whenever you feel the pressure building, your body will relax, and you will feel a sense of control." This helps the person reprogram their automatic stress response, so they can handle pressure without becoming overwhelmed.
- **Calming Visualization:** Visualization techniques can also be used as post-hypnotic suggestions. The hypnotist might guide the individual to imagine a peaceful place—such as a beach, forest, or quiet garden—and suggest that, whenever they visualize this place in the future, they will automatically experience the same relaxation and calmness they felt during the session. This mental imagery serves as a trigger for relaxation, helping the individual to tap into a peaceful state whenever needed.
- **Positive Affirmations:** Post-hypnotic suggestions may also include affirmations aimed at changing the individual's mindset toward stress. For example, a person might be given the suggestion: "You are resilient and capable of handling anything that comes your way," or "You are in control of your stress, and you can easily manage any challenge." These affirmations help to reprogram the subconscious to view stress from a more empowering and manageable perspective.

3. Benefits of Post-Hypnotic Suggestions for Stress Relief

Post-hypnotic suggestions for stress relief have a number of key benefits, both immediate and long-term:

- **Reduced Anxiety:** Once post-hypnotic suggestions are embedded in the subconscious mind, they help the individual respond to anxiety triggers in a calmer way. Rather than spiraling into stress or panic, the individual automatically taps into their new coping mechanisms, leading to less anxiety and more emotional stability.
- **Increased Sense of Control:** By reprogramming the subconscious mind to handle stress in healthier ways, post-hypnotic suggestions help individuals feel more in control of their emotional reactions. This sense of control can be empowering, reducing the feeling of being overwhelmed and helping the individual approach challenges with confidence.

- **Improved Relaxation:** With repeated exposure to relaxation triggers and calming suggestions, individuals can enter a state of deep relaxation more easily and frequently, even without hypnosis. This ability to relax on command can be incredibly helpful in reducing stress during daily activities or high-pressure situations.
- **Lasting Change:** Unlike simple stress management techniques that may only work in the moment, post-hypnotic suggestions can produce lasting change. Over time, these suggestions become internalized, leading to automatic changes in the individual's behavior and thought patterns. As a result, stress management becomes ingrained in the individual's subconscious, making it easier to cope with stress in the future.

. Practical Applications of Post-Hypnotic Suggestions for Stress

Post-hypnotic suggestions can be applied to a variety of real-life stressors, including work-related pressure, family stress, social anxiety, and more. For instance, someone who experiences stress at work may receive post-hypnotic suggestions to remain calm and composed in meetings, take breaks to relax, and manage deadlines without feeling overwhelmed. Similarly, someone who experiences social anxiety might be given suggestions to feel confident and at ease when meeting new people or speaking in public.

These suggestions can also be used in combination with other stress management techniques, such as mindfulness or deep breathing exercises, to provide a more comprehensive approach to stress relief. As the individual practices and reinforces the suggestions, their stress responses begin to change, leading to a more resilient and relaxed way of coping with challenges.

. Self-Hypnosis and Post-Hypnotic Suggestions

One of the most valuable aspects of post-hypnotic suggestions is that they can be used outside of formal hypnosis sessions. With practice, individuals can learn to induce a relaxed, self-hypnotic state and reinforce their post-hypnotic suggestions on their own. This empowers individuals to take control of their stress relief, even in situations where they don't have access to a hypnotherapist. Self-hypnosis allows people to integrate relaxation techniques and positive suggestions into their daily lives, making it easier to manage stress whenever it arises.

Conclusion

Post-hypnotic suggestions are a powerful tool for stress relief, enabling individuals to reprogram their subconscious mind and develop healthier responses to stress. By creating triggers for relaxation, promoting positive affirmations, and helping individuals feel more in control, these suggestions provide both immediate and lasting benefits. Whether used in a formal hypnotherapy session or through self-hypnosis, post-hypnotic suggestions can help individuals manage stress with greater ease, improving emotional well-being and overall quality of life.

Hypnosis for Anxiety and Depression

Hypnosis has increasingly been recognized as an effective therapeutic tool for managing anxiety and depression. Both conditions, often deeply intertwined, can cause significant emotional and physical distress, leading individuals to feel overwhelmed, helpless, and unable to control their emotional states. While conventional treatments like medication and psychotherapy are widely used, hypnosis offers an alternative approach by working directly with the subconscious mind to address the root causes of these mental health issues and reshape the individual's response to stressors.

The process of hypnosis involves guiding an individual into a deeply relaxed state where they become more receptive to suggestions. In this heightened state of awareness, the subconscious mind is more accessible, allowing the therapist to introduce ideas and suggestions that can change negative thought patterns and emotional responses. By tapping into this subconscious realm, hypnosis can help individuals address the underlying factors contributing to their anxiety and depression, shifting their thoughts, beliefs, and behaviors toward more positive and constructive outcomes.

How Hypnosis Works for Anxiety and Depression

Anxiety and depression are often driven by distorted thinking patterns, unresolved emotional trauma, or negative beliefs about oneself and the world. These thought patterns are usually held in the subconscious mind, which operates automatically and can be difficult to change through conscious effort alone. Hypnosis, by bypassing the critical, conscious mind, helps to access and reprogram these negative thought patterns, allowing individuals to experience a shift in how they perceive and react to stressors.

1. **Reframing Negative Thoughts**
   One of the most effective ways hypnosis addresses anxiety and depression is by reframing negative thought patterns. For example, someone suffering from anxiety may have constant worry about the future, believing they won't be able to handle challenges. A hypnotherapist may guide the individual to see themselves as capable and resourceful in stressful situations. Over time, these positive suggestions can rewire the subconscious mind, replacing worry with confidence and calmness.
2. **Changing Negative Beliefs**
   Hypnosis can also help individuals address deeply rooted negative beliefs about themselves. People with depression often harbor feelings of worthlessness or

hopelessness, which only perpetuate their emotional state. Hypnotherapy can suggest more empowering beliefs, such as, "I am worthy of happiness," or "I have the strength to overcome challenges." Repeating these suggestions during hypnosis can gradually replace old, negative beliefs with healthier, more balanced perspectives.

3. **Relaxation and Stress Reduction**
   Both anxiety and depression are often associated with heightened physical tension, such as tight muscles, shallow breathing, and a racing heart. Hypnosis is known for its ability to induce deep relaxation, which can help reduce the physical symptoms of anxiety and depression. During a session, the individual is guided into a calm state, often through techniques like progressive relaxation or guided imagery. Once relaxed, the body is better able to release tension, and the mind can more effectively process and release negative emotions.

The Benefits of Hypnosis for Anxiety and Depression

1. **Reduced Anxiety**
   Anxiety often manifests as excessive worry, tension, and a feeling of being out of control. Hypnosis helps by teaching the subconscious mind to adopt healthier ways of responding to anxiety triggers. Techniques such as breathing exercises, mental imagery, and positive affirmations are used to reduce feelings of fear or unease. Many individuals report feeling more in control of their anxiety after hypnosis, finding it easier to remain calm during stressful situations.

2. **Enhanced Emotional Resilience**
   Depression can create a sense of emotional paralysis, where individuals feel unable to cope with life's challenges. Hypnosis can help build emotional resilience by encouraging the subconscious mind to access inner strength and self-compassion. By helping individuals develop a positive mindset and belief in their ability to cope, hypnosis fosters emotional flexibility and resilience, making it easier for individuals to handle life's ups and downs.

3. **Improved Sleep**
   Anxiety and depression are often linked to sleep disturbances, which can worsen both conditions. Hypnosis promotes relaxation, allowing the individual to let go of intrusive thoughts that might interfere with sleep. By using specific hypnotic suggestions to calm the mind and body, sleep quality can improve significantly, leading to better rest and overall emotional well-being.

4. **Breaking the Cycle of Negative Thinking**
   Anxiety and depression are often cyclical in nature. Negative thoughts lead to feelings of hopelessness, which in turn fuel more negative thinking. Hypnosis can disrupt this cycle by introducing positive thoughts, feelings of relaxation, and suggestions that promote a more hopeful outlook. The more these suggestions are repeated during hypnosis, the more the subconscious mind begins to adopt them as truths, helping to break the cycle of negativity.

One of the most empowering aspects of hypnosis is the ability for individuals to learn self-hypnosis techniques. While professional hypnosis sessions are effective, many people with anxiety and depression benefit from learning how to use self-hypnosis in their daily lives. Through guided practice, individuals can teach themselves to enter a relaxed state and access positive suggestions anytime they need to manage stress, reduce anxiety, or overcome depressive thoughts.

Self-hypnosis techniques for managing anxiety and depression might include:

- **Progressive Relaxation:** Focusing on each part of the body to progressively relax muscles, reducing physical tension associated with anxiety or depression.
- **Visualization:** Using mental imagery to create peaceful, calming scenes or positive outcomes, which can replace anxious or negative thoughts.
- **Affirmations:** Repeating positive, empowering statements to challenge the negative beliefs associated with depression, such as, "I am in control of my thoughts," or "I can handle whatever comes my way."

These self-hypnosis tools can help individuals feel more empowered to manage their mental health and alleviate symptoms of anxiety and depression on their own.

Scientific Evidence Supporting Hypnosis for Anxiety and Depression

While hypnosis has long been used in therapeutic contexts, recent studies have further validated its effectiveness in treating anxiety and depression. Research shows that hypnosis can help reduce anxiety by promoting relaxation and altering the way the brain processes stress. A study published in the *International Journal of Clinical and Experimental Hypnosis* found that hypnosis significantly reduced anxiety levels in individuals with generalized anxiety disorder.

Similarly, hypnosis has been shown to improve mood and reduce depressive symptoms. A meta-analysis published in the *Journal of Clinical Psychology* found that hypnosis was effective in alleviating symptoms of depression, especially when combined with other therapeutic approaches, such as cognitive-behavioral therapy.

Conclusion

Hypnosis offers a valuable approach for managing anxiety and depression by working directly with the subconscious mind. By reframing negative thought patterns, releasing emotional blocks, and promoting deep relaxation, hypnosis helps individuals feel more in control of their emotions and better equipped to handle life's challenges. Whether used in professional sessions or through self-hypnosis techniques, it provides a powerful tool for lasting change, fostering emotional resilience, and improving overall mental well-being.

How Hypnosis Helps Combat Anxiety

Anxiety often manifests as a constant state of worry, tension, and fear, making it difficult for individuals to feel at ease in everyday situations. Whether it's the fear of social interactions, performance anxiety, or a general sense of impending doom, anxiety can be overwhelming. Traditional treatments such as medication and psychotherapy are effective for many, but hypnosis offers a unique approach by addressing the root causes of anxiety in the subconscious mind, providing long-term relief through relaxation and cognitive shifts.

Hypnosis works by guiding individuals into a relaxed, focused state, where the subconscious mind becomes more open to suggestion. During this time, a trained hypnotherapist can help the individual reframe anxious thoughts, reduce stress responses, and install healthier coping mechanisms. By engaging the subconscious, hypnosis allows people to bypass the conscious mind's habitual patterns of overthinking and worrying, replacing them with calming and empowering thoughts.

How Hypnosis Relieves Anxiety

1. **Promoting Deep Relaxation**

One of the most immediate benefits of hypnosis is its ability to induce deep relaxation. Anxiety is often accompanied by physical symptoms like a racing heart, shallow breathing, muscle tension, and heightened alertness—responses rooted in the body's fight-or-flight mechanism. Hypnosis helps to counteract this by activating the parasympathetic nervous system, which promotes relaxation and reduces the physiological effects of anxiety. Techniques such as progressive muscle relaxation, deep breathing, and guided imagery are commonly used in hypnosis to lower the body's stress levels.

When in a relaxed state, the body is able to rest and reset, allowing the individual to experience relief from the physical discomfort of anxiety. Over time, this relaxation response becomes more readily available, even outside of hypnosis, helping the person to cope with anxiety-provoking situations in their daily life.

2. **Reframing Negative Thought Patterns**

Anxiety is often driven by negative thinking patterns—such as catastrophic thoughts, excessive worry about the future, or an irrational fear of situations that may never occur. In a hypnotic state, the conscious mind is relaxed, making it easier to access the subconscious, where these thought patterns are stored. Hypnotherapists can use direct suggestions and visualization techniques to help individuals challenge and reframe their anxious thoughts.

For example, someone who experiences anxiety about public speaking might receive suggestions like, "You are calm and confident in front of others," or "You enjoy the experience of speaking and engaging with an audience." By repeatedly reinforcing these suggestions, hypnosis helps to overwrite old beliefs with more positive, adaptive thoughts, thereby reducing anxiety related to public speaking or other feared situations.

3. Changing Automatic Stress Responses

Anxiety often leads to automatic, knee-jerk stress responses, such as increased heart rate, shallow breathing, or a sense of impending doom. These responses are hardwired into the brain, but hypnosis can reprogram the subconscious to react differently. Through post-hypnotic suggestions, individuals can learn to respond to triggers with calmness and control rather than panic or fear.

For instance, a person who experiences anxiety when entering crowded places might be given the suggestion, "When you enter a crowded space, you will feel calm and at ease." The subconscious mind internalizes this suggestion, and over time, the individual's response to crowded spaces becomes one of calmness rather than anxiety.

4. Addressing Root Causes of Anxiety

Many individuals with chronic anxiety have underlying causes—such as unresolved trauma, past experiences, or deeply ingrained fears—that contribute to their current state. Hypnosis can help uncover and address these root causes by guiding the individual into a relaxed state where repressed memories or emotions may surface. By revisiting and reframing these experiences, the individual can release emotional blockages that may have been contributing to their anxiety.

For example, someone who experienced childhood trauma may find that unresolved feelings of fear and insecurity are still influencing their adult life. Through hypnosis, they can reframe these memories, gain a sense of closure, and let go of the fear that continues to affect them. This process can be incredibly therapeutic, helping the individual to heal and break free from the cycle of anxiety.

5. Instilling Confidence and Self-Efficacy

Anxiety often stems from a lack of confidence or a belief that one is incapable of handling stressful situations. Hypnosis can help individuals rebuild self-confidence by reinforcing a belief in their own abilities and resilience. Through positive affirmations and visualizations, a person can be guided to see themselves as capable, calm, and in control when faced with challenges. For example, the therapist may suggest, "You are fully capable of managing stress," or "You have the strength to handle any situation with calm and composure."

Over time, these suggestions build the individual's self-efficacy, helping them to trust in their ability to cope with anxiety and navigate stressful situations with greater ease.

6. Empowering Mind-Body Connection

A crucial aspect of managing anxiety is understanding the mind-body connection and learning how thoughts and emotions influence physical states. Hypnosis encourages individuals to become more attuned to their bodies, recognizing when anxiety is building up and learning to interrupt the stress response before it becomes overwhelming. Techniques such as guided relaxation, breath work, and body scanning can help individuals become more aware of physical tension and develop tools to release it in real-time.

By strengthening this connection, individuals can reduce the physical symptoms of anxiety and manage their emotional responses more effectively, both during and after a hypnosis session.

The Benefits of Hypnosis for Anxiety

- **Long-term Relief:** Unlike temporary fixes such as medication, hypnosis works to reprogram the subconscious mind, helping to create lasting changes in behavior, thought patterns, and emotional responses.
- **Fewer Side Effects:** Hypnosis is a natural and non-invasive method for managing anxiety, offering an alternative to medications that often come with unwanted side effects.
- **Increased Self-Awareness:** Hypnosis allows individuals to gain insight into their thought patterns and emotional triggers, empowering them to take more control over their anxiety and mental health.
- **Personalized Treatment:** Hypnotherapy is tailored to the individual's unique experiences and triggers, making it a highly personalized and effective treatment option.

Conclusion

Hypnosis offers a powerful approach for combating anxiety by addressing the root causes, reprogramming negative thought patterns, and promoting relaxation and self-confidence. By working with the subconscious mind, hypnosis provides individuals with the tools to manage their anxiety in a more effective and lasting way. Whether through professional hypnotherapy or self-hypnosis techniques, many individuals have found relief from the overwhelming grip of anxiety, leading to improved mental well-being and a greater sense of control over their emotions.

Dealing with Depression Through Hypnosis

Depression is a pervasive condition that affects millions of people worldwide, often making even the most basic daily activities feel insurmountable. Characterized by persistent feelings of sadness, hopelessness, and a lack of motivation, depression can be difficult to manage through conventional treatments alone. While therapy and medication are common methods of treatment, hypnosis offers an alternative, or complementary, approach that targets the subconscious mind to address the root causes of depressive symptoms and help reshape thought patterns.

At its core, hypnosis involves guiding individuals into a deeply relaxed state, allowing them to access their subconscious minds more easily. In this state, the conscious mind is less active, and the individual becomes more receptive to positive suggestions and therapeutic interventions. Through hypnosis, it's possible to reframe negative thought patterns, address unresolved emotional conflicts, and instill new, healthier beliefs and behaviors that support long-term healing from depression.

How Hypnosis Helps Combat Depression

1. **Reprogramming Negative Thought Patterns**

One of the hallmark features of depression is persistent negative thinking, where individuals often see themselves, their lives, and their futures through a lens of hopelessness or worthlessness. The subconscious mind holds onto these negative beliefs, reinforcing them over time. Hypnosis offers a way to access the subconscious directly and change these deeply ingrained thought patterns.

During a session, a trained hypnotherapist can help individuals identify and challenge these negative beliefs. For instance, someone who feels unworthy or incapable may be given suggestions like, "You are worthy of love and happiness" or "You have the strength to overcome challenges." Repeated exposure to these positive affirmations, particularly in a deeply relaxed state, can help rewire the subconscious mind, replacing self-doubt with self-compassion and hope.

2. **Releasing Emotional Trauma**

Many people with depression carry unresolved emotional trauma, whether from past relationships, loss, or childhood experiences. These unresolved issues can manifest as feelings of sadness, guilt, or shame, which contribute to the depressive state. Hypnosis can help individuals access and process these repressed emotions in a safe, controlled manner.

Through guided visualization or regression techniques, a hypnotherapist can help individuals revisit past experiences, process the associated emotions, and release the emotional burden. By confronting and reframing these memories in the subconscious, individuals can gain closure and healing, ultimately lifting the weight of the past and reducing its impact on their current emotional state.

3. Promoting Relaxation and Stress Reduction

Chronic stress and tension often exacerbate depressive symptoms, creating a vicious cycle that becomes difficult to break. Hypnosis can induce deep relaxation, which counteracts the body's stress response and helps reduce the physical manifestations of depression, such as fatigue, muscle tension, and insomnia.

By encouraging deep breathing, muscle relaxation, and visualization of peaceful, calming environments, hypnosis helps activate the body's parasympathetic nervous system, promoting a state of calm. This relaxation not only provides immediate relief from stress but can also improve sleep patterns, increase energy, and support overall emotional well-being.

4. Increasing Motivation and Goal-Oriented Thinking

Depression often results in a lack of motivation, making it challenging for individuals to engage in daily activities or pursue goals. Hypnosis can help break this cycle by increasing motivation and encouraging goal-oriented thinking. A trained hypnotherapist can guide individuals to visualize their goals, whether they are related to personal, social, or professional aspirations.

Through hypnotic suggestions, individuals can imagine themselves achieving their goals and experiencing success, which in turn boosts confidence and motivation. Hypnosis can also encourage individuals to take small, manageable steps toward their goals, which can build momentum and create a sense of accomplishment, gradually overcoming the inertia that often accompanies depression.

5. Improving Self-Esteem and Self-Worth

A significant aspect of depression is the feeling of low self-esteem or unworthiness. Hypnosis can help individuals reframe their self-image by introducing positive ffirmations and suggestions that promote self-love and self-compassion. For example, ndividuals may be guided to visualize themselves as strong, confident, and deserving of appiness.

By reinforcing these positive thoughts and building a more supportive self-image, ypnosis helps individuals cultivate a healthier sense of self-worth, which is essential for vercoming depression. With greater self-esteem, individuals are more likely to engage n positive actions, form healthy relationships, and break free from the emotional barriers hat depression creates.

6. **Instilling Coping Mechanisms**

Iypnosis can also teach individuals effective coping strategies for dealing with future epressive episodes or stressful situations. These techniques are often learned during the ypnotic state and can include relaxation techniques, positive self-talk, and methods for hallenging negative thought patterns. Over time, these coping mechanisms become utomatic responses, helping individuals to manage their depression and prevent it from ecoming overwhelming.

'or example, individuals may be taught to use deep breathing or visualization when they egin to feel overwhelmed by depressive thoughts or emotions. These tools can provide mmediate relief and help individuals regain a sense of control over their emotional state.

he Benefits of Hypnosis for Depression

- **Non-invasive and Natural:** Hypnosis is a non-medical, drug-free approach to treating depression, making it a safe option for those who prefer to avoid medications or experience negative side effects from them.
- **Personalized Treatment:** Each session can be tailored to the individual's specific experiences and needs. Whether it's addressing past trauma, boosting motivation, or reprogramming negative thought patterns, hypnosis can be adapted to address the unique factors contributing to each person's depression.
- **Long-Term Relief:** While medication can offer short-term relief from depressive symptoms, hypnosis works to address the root causes of depression, reprogramming the subconscious mind for long-lasting change. Many individuals experience sustained improvement in their mood and emotional well-being after undergoing hypnotherapy.
- **Empowerment and Self-Efficacy:** Hypnosis helps individuals develop a stronger sense of self-efficacy, empowering them to take control of their emotional health. By learning relaxation techniques, self-hypnosis, and positive thinking strategies, individuals can continue to manage their depression on their own long after the sessions have ended.

Research on the efficacy of hypnosis for treating depression has shown promising results. A study published in *Psychological Reports* found that individuals who underwent hypnotherapy experienced significant reductions in depressive symptoms compared to those who received standard cognitive-behavioral therapy (CBT) or no treatment at all. Other studies have shown that hypnosis can be effective in addressing the underlying causes of depression, such as trauma or negative thinking patterns, leading to long-term improvements in mental health.

Conclusion

Hypnosis offers a unique, effective approach to managing and overcoming depression by addressing the root causes of the condition in the subconscious mind. Through relaxation, reframing negative beliefs, releasing emotional trauma, and instilling healthier coping mechanisms, hypnosis empowers individuals to regain control over their emotional health. Whether used alongside other treatments or as a stand-alone therapy, hypnosis provides a natural, non-invasive way to reduce depressive symptoms and foster long-term healing and well-being.

Studies Supporting Hypnosis for Anxiety and Depression

Numerous studies have examined the effectiveness of hypnosis in treating anxiety and depression, showing promising results across different settings and populations. While hypnosis is often used in conjunction with other therapies, research consistently highlights its potential as a standalone treatment, particularly for individuals looking for non-invasive alternatives to medications. By accessing the subconscious mind, hypnosis allows for deep emotional processing, relaxation, and reprogramming of negative thought patterns, all of which contribute to its ability to alleviate symptoms of both anxiety and depression.

Studies on Hypnosis for Anxiety

A 2016 meta-analysis published in *International Journal of Clinical and Experimental Hypnosis* examined 13 randomized controlled trials to assess the efficacy of hypnosis for reducing anxiety. The study concluded that hypnosis produced a medium to large effect size for anxiety reduction, with improvements maintained over time. Hypnosis was found to be particularly effective for situational anxiety, such as public speaking, as well as generalized anxiety disorder (GAD). The study also noted that hypnosis often led to more sustainable results when compared to other anxiety treatments, like cognitive-behavioral therapy (CBT) or pharmacological interventions.

Another notable study, published in *American Journal of Clinical Hypnosis* (2017), explored the effects of hypnosis on anxiety in patients undergoing medical procedures. The researchers found that individuals who underwent hypnosis before and during procedures reported significantly lower anxiety levels compared to those who received standard care. The participants in the hypnosis group also experienced lower levels of pain, demonstrating how hypnosis can not only address psychological distress but also affect physical symptoms associated with anxiety.

Studies on Hypnosis for Depression

Hypnosis has also shown promise as a treatment for depression, particularly in helping individuals break free from negative thought patterns and unresolved emotional issues. A study published in *Journal of Consulting and Clinical Psychology* (2010) involved 128 individuals diagnosed with major depressive disorder. Participants were randomly assigned to receive either hypnosis or a placebo treatment. The results showed that the hypnosis group experienced a greater reduction in depressive symptoms, with improvements in both mood and quality of life compared to the placebo group.

Similarly, a study in *Clinical Psychology & Psychotherapy* (2013) explored the effectiveness of hypnosis in conjunction with cognitive-behavioral therapy (CBT) for individuals with treatment-resistant depression. The research team found that combining hypnosis with CBT led to more significant reductions in depressive symptoms than CBT alone. The study suggested that hypnosis may enhance the cognitive restructuring aspect of therapy, helping individuals internalize positive changes more effectively.

Effectiveness of Hypnosis in Addressing Both Anxiety and Depression

A 2016 review published in *Psychological Reports* synthesized findings from several studies to investigate the impact of hypnosis on both anxiety and depression. The review concluded that hypnosis could serve as an effective treatment for both conditions, either alone or as a complementary therapy. Participants in studies showed improvements in mood, emotional regulation, and stress reduction following hypnosis interventions. The review also highlighted that hypnosis helped reduce rumination and negative thought cycles, which are often characteristic of both anxiety and depression.

Furthermore, a study published in *British Journal of Clinical Psychology* (2015) examined the combined effects of hypnosis on patients suffering from both anxiety and depression. The researchers found that hypnosis significantly alleviated symptoms of both conditions, with participants experiencing greater relaxation, improved sleep, and decreased emotional distress. The study emphasized that hypnosis's ability to access and reframe subconscious thought patterns could address the root causes of both anxiety and depression simultaneously, leading to more comprehensive improvements in mental health.

Mechanisms Behind Hypnosis' Effectiveness

The positive outcomes reported in these studies are believed to be due to hypnosis's ability to tap into the subconscious mind, where negative thought patterns, emotional trauma, and unresolved conflicts often reside. Hypnosis promotes a deep state of relaxation, allowing individuals to reframe destructive beliefs and past experiences. Suggestions made during hypnosis can help individuals reprogram the brain to respond to stress, anxiety, and depressive thoughts in healthier ways.

Research published in *The Lancet Psychiatry* (2014) indicated that the effectiveness of hypnosis for treating anxiety and depression is partly due to its ability to reduce physiological arousal and activate the parasympathetic nervous system, which is responsible for relaxation. By reducing the body's fight-or-flight response, hypnosis counteracts the physical symptoms associated with both anxiety and depression, such as racing heart rates, muscle tension, and insomnia. This physiological calming effect can help individuals better manage their emotions and cope with stress more effectively.

Limitations of Current Research

While the studies supporting hypnosis for anxiety and depression are encouraging, there are some limitations that should be considered. Many studies on hypnosis are small-scale or rely on self-reported data, which can be prone to bias. Additionally, the effectiveness of hypnosis may vary depending on the individual's susceptibility to the technique. Not everyone is equally responsive to hypnosis, and results can differ based on factors such as the skill of the hypnotherapist, the patient's openness to the process, and the nature of the anxiety or depression being treated.

There is also a need for more large-scale, long-term studies to determine how hypnosis compares to other established treatments, such as cognitive-behavioral therapy or medication. While early findings are promising, more rigorous research is required to fully understand the long-term benefits and optimal applications of hypnosis for anxiety and depression.

Conclusion

The research supporting the use of hypnosis for treating anxiety and depression is compelling, with studies showing that hypnosis can lead to significant reductions in symptoms and help individuals address the underlying causes of their emotional distress. Through techniques like reframing negative thought patterns, reducing stress, and promoting relaxation, hypnosis offers a powerful tool for individuals seeking non-pharmacological treatments for anxiety and depression. Although further research is needed to solidify its place in mainstream therapeutic practices, the existing body of evidence suggests that hypnosis can be an effective and valuable addition to the mental health treatment toolbox.

Hypnosis and Pain Management

Pain, whether chronic or acute, can have a debilitating effect on both physical and emotional well-being. Traditional pain management techniques often involve medications or physical therapies, but hypnosis offers an alternative or complementary approach that targets the mind-body connection to help reduce the perception of pain. By inducing a deeply relaxed state, hypnosis can enable individuals to access the subconscious mind, allowing them to alter their experience of pain and foster healing.

The Science Behind Hypnosis and Pain Management

Pain is not just a physical sensation; it is heavily influenced by psychological factors such as stress, emotions, and past experiences. When we experience pain, the brain processes it and triggers a response in the nervous system. This response involves the release of chemicals like endorphins and cortisol, which affect how we perceive and respond to discomfort.

Hypnosis works by influencing these processes. In a relaxed state, individuals are more receptive to suggestions that can alter their pain perception. By accessing the subconscious mind, hypnosis can shift how the brain processes pain signals, often reducing the intensity or unpleasantness of the experience. This can be particularly useful in managing both acute and chronic pain, such as that associated with conditions like arthritis, fibromyalgia, migraines, or post-surgical recovery.

How Hypnosis Helps in Pain Reduction

1. **Reducing the Emotional Impact of Pain**

Pain is often exacerbated by emotional factors such as anxiety, fear, and stress. These emotional responses can amplify the perception of pain and make it feel more overwhelming. Hypnosis helps address the emotional component of pain by promoting relaxation and reducing stress. In a deeply relaxed state, the subconscious mind becomes more receptive to positive suggestions, such as calming thoughts or feelings of comfort, which can reduce the emotional distress associated with pain.

2. **Altered Pain Perception**

During hypnosis, individuals are guided into a trance-like state that allows them to detach from the immediate sensations of pain. In this state, the brain becomes less focused on the physical discomfort, and the individual may be able to perceive pain as less intense or even eliminate it entirely for a period. A common hypnotic technique involves guiding individuals to visualize the pain as a shape, color, or temperature and then instructing them to alter its characteristics (e.g., changing the color to a soothing hue or making the sensation cooler and less intense). These mental shifts can make the pain feel more manageable.

3. Empowering Self-Control Over Pain

Hypnosis can also teach individuals how to use their minds to control pain in real-time. This self-hypnosis technique empowers individuals to alter their perception of pain whenever it arises. Patients can learn to induce a relaxed state and use mental imagery or affirmations to reduce pain intensity. For example, someone suffering from chronic back pain may visualize a warm, soothing light easing the discomfort or mentally tell themselves that the pain is temporary and under their control. Over time, these self-regulation techniques can be used independently, providing lasting relief.

4. Promoting Healing and Recovery

In addition to reducing pain perception, hypnosis has been shown to promote faster healing. Research suggests that hypnosis can enhance the body's natural healing mechanisms by improving circulation, reducing inflammation, and promoting relaxation. For example, in post-surgical recovery, hypnosis has been found to reduce both pain and the need for pain medication. It also helps speed up recovery times by encouraging the body to focus energy on healing rather than on the sensation of discomfort.

5. Managing Chronic Pain

Chronic pain, such as that experienced in conditions like fibromyalgia, arthritis, or neuropathy, is often not fully responsive to conventional treatments. For people with chronic pain, hypnosis offers a non-invasive, drug-free way to manage ongoing discomfort. Several studies have demonstrated that patients with chronic pain can experience significant reductions in pain intensity, frequency, and distress when using hypnosis as part of a treatment plan.

For example, a study published in *The International Journal of Clinical and Experimental Hypnosis* found that individuals with chronic pain who underwent hypnosis experienced a significant decrease in pain intensity and a reduction in the emotional distress caused by their pain. This study also showed that the effects of hypnosis were long-lasting, with participants reporting continued pain relief even after the sessions had concluded.

6. **Pain Management in Medical Procedures**

Hypnosis has also been successfully used in medical settings to manage pain during and after procedures. In cases where patients are undergoing minor surgeries, dental work, or diagnostic procedures, hypnosis can help reduce the need for anesthetics and pain medications. Studies have found that individuals who underwent hypnosis during medical procedures reported lower pain levels, reduced anxiety, and quicker recovery times compared to those who only received conventional treatments.

For example, in a study published in *The Lancet* (2000), patients who used hypnosis to manage pain during dental procedures required less local anesthesia and reported significantly lower levels of pain and anxiety. This approach not only minimized the need for medication but also promoted a more relaxed and positive experience for the patients.

Scientific Support for Hypnosis in Pain Management

The scientific community has increasingly acknowledged the effectiveness of hypnosis in pain management. Numerous clinical trials and meta-analyses have demonstrated that hypnosis is a powerful tool for reducing both acute and chronic pain. A meta-analysis conducted by the *American Psychological Association* (2015) reviewed over 20 studies on the use of hypnosis for pain relief and found that it consistently resulted in significant reductions in pain intensity across various conditions, including burn pain, cancer pain, and post-operative pain.

Another study published in *Pain* (2000) examined the effects of hypnosis on individuals with chronic pain due to rheumatoid arthritis. The results showed that patients who underwent hypnosis experienced a 40% reduction in pain intensity and a 50% reduction in emotional distress related to the pain. These findings suggest that hypnosis can help alleviate the suffering associated with chronic pain by addressing both the physical and emotional components of the experience.

Hypnosis vs. Traditional Pain Management

One of the most significant advantages of using hypnosis for pain management is that it is non-invasive and free from the side effects commonly associated with pain medications. Many pain medications, especially opioids, carry the risk of addiction, tolerance, and long-term health complications. Hypnosis, on the other hand, is a safe and natural technique that can be used in conjunction with other pain management strategies or as a standalone therapy.

Furthermore, hypnosis does not require the use of pharmaceuticals, making it an attractive option for individuals who may be sensitive to medications or those who prefer to avoid drugs altogether. This makes hypnosis particularly valuable for patients with chronic pain who need ongoing relief but wish to reduce their reliance on medications.

Limitations and Considerations

Although hypnosis can be highly effective for pain management, it may not work for everyone. Individuals who are less susceptible to hypnosis may not experience the same degree of pain reduction as those who are more responsive to the technique. Additionally, hypnosis should not be considered a cure for pain conditions but rather a tool to help manage and reduce pain symptoms. It is most effective when used as part of a comprehensive pain management plan that includes other therapies, such as physical therapy, medication, or lifestyle changes.

Conclusion

Hypnosis offers a unique and effective approach to managing pain, addressing both the physical and emotional aspects of pain perception. By inducing a state of relaxation and promoting the use of mental imagery and self-regulation, hypnosis can help reduce pain intensity, improve emotional well-being, and speed up recovery. Whether used to manage chronic pain, support medical procedures, or assist in post-surgical recovery, hypnosis provides a safe and non-invasive alternative or complement to traditional pain management methods. As more research continues to highlight its effectiveness, hypnosis is becoming an increasingly valuable tool in pain management.

The Mind-body Connection

The mind and body are intricately connected, with each influencing the other in ways that scientists and medical professionals are still uncovering. This dynamic relationship forms the foundation of many psychological and physiological processes, including how we experience stress, manage pain, and even heal from illness. The mind-body connection is particularly significant in the context of hypnosis, a therapeutic practice that taps into the subconscious mind to produce physical and emotional changes. By understanding the ways in which mental and physical states are interlinked, we can better appreciate how hypnosis works to promote well-being and address various health concerns.

The Science Behind the Mind-Body Connection

The mind-body connection refers to the powerful interactions between our thoughts, emotions, and physical health. These interactions are mediated through the nervous system, hormones, and immune responses. For instance, when a person experiences stress, the brain signals the release of stress hormones like cortisol, which triggers the "fight or flight" response. This, in turn, can affect the body's organs, muscles, and overall immune function.

Conversely, the state of the body can influence mental states. For example, chronic pain or illness can lead to depression, anxiety, and feelings of helplessness. Similarly, poor posture or physical discomfort can lead to emotional stress or cognitive strain. The integration of mind and body explains why conditions such as chronic pain, stress, and even anxiety or depression are often interrelated.

How Hypnosis Utilizes the Mind-Body Connection

Hypnosis is a tool that capitalizes on the mind-body connection by inducing a deeply relaxed state in which individuals become highly suggestible and aware of their thoughts, emotions, and physical sensations. During hypnosis, the mind becomes more open to suggestions that can influence both mental and physical states. This allows individuals to alter their perception of pain, reduce stress, and even address physical conditions that are exacerbated by psychological factors.

One of the key mechanisms behind hypnosis is its ability to shift the focus of attention. By guiding a person's attention inward, hypnosis helps them tune out external distractions and focus on mental imagery or relaxation techniques. This concentration allows the subconscious mind to become more receptive to suggestions for healing, relaxation, or behavioral change, which can lead to noticeable changes in both mental and physical states.

Impact of Hypnosis on Physical Health

Research into hypnosis has shown that it can be used to treat various physical conditions by harnessing the mind-body connection. For example, hypnosis has been used to manage pain, alleviate symptoms of irritable bowel syndrome (IBS), and reduce the severity of conditions like migraines. In these cases, hypnosis works by altering the way the brain perceives and processes physical sensations. Suggestions made during hypnosis can influence pain thresholds, lower the body's stress response, and promote a sense of calm or well-being.

Hypnosis has also been found to enhance the body's natural healing processes. In post-surgical recovery, hypnosis can reduce the need for pain medications, promote faster tissue healing, and lessen the incidence of complications. By reducing stress and anxiety, hypnosis creates a more favorable environment for the body to recover and repair itself. Studies have shown that individuals who use hypnosis during surgery or medical procedures report less pain and quicker recovery times compared to those who do not.

Psychological Impact and Emotional Healing

Beyond its physical benefits, hypnosis plays a significant role in emotional healing by helping individuals access the subconscious mind. Many emotional issues, such as unresolved trauma, phobias, or deep-seated anxiety, have roots in the subconscious, where they can influence thoughts and behaviors without conscious awareness. Hypnosis allows individuals to explore and address these hidden emotional triggers, leading to long-term healing and improved mental health.

For example, someone dealing with chronic stress may use hypnosis to identify the underlying thoughts and beliefs that are contributing to their stress response. Hypnotic suggestions can then help reframe these beliefs, leading to a reduction in stress and anxiety. This change in mental state can, in turn, have a profound effect on the physical body, lowering blood pressure, reducing muscle tension, and improving overall health.

The Role of Visualization in Healing

Visualization is a common technique used in hypnosis that leverages the mind-body connection. In a hypnotic trance, individuals can visualize healing imagery—such as imagining the body's cells repairing themselves or picturing pain melting away. These mental images can trigger physical changes in the body by influencing the nervous system and immune function. Scientific studies have shown that mental imagery can boost immune responses, reduce inflammation, and help the body respond more effectively to injury or illness.

In fact, athletes and individuals undergoing medical treatments often use visualization techniques to improve performance and accelerate healing. For example, cancer patients may visualize their body's immune cells attacking cancerous cells, while athletes might visualize themselves succeeding in their sport. This form of mental training, often incorporated into hypnotherapy, can harness the power of the mind to enhance physical outcomes.

Mind-Body Approaches in Chronic Illness and Pain

One of the most compelling applications of hypnosis in the mind-body connection is its ability to address chronic conditions where psychological and physical factors are closely intertwined. Chronic pain conditions, such as fibromyalgia, arthritis, and back pain, often involve both physical discomfort and emotional stress, creating a cycle that can be difficult to break. Hypnosis helps break this cycle by reducing the emotional distress associated with pain and altering how pain is experienced in the brain.

In a study published in *The Journal of Pain* (2007), researchers found that individuals with chronic pain who underwent hypnosis experienced significant reductions in pain intensity and emotional distress compared to those who received conventional treatments alone. The mind-body connection in these cases is key—by altering the brain's perception of pain through hypnosis, patients experience not only reduced discomfort but also emotional relief, breaking the cycle of stress and pain.

Similarly, conditions like irritable bowel syndrome (IBS) and tension headaches, which have a strong psychological component, can be treated using hypnosis. Studies have shown that hypnosis can reduce symptoms of IBS, such as bloating, cramping, and irregular bowel movements, by addressing stress, anxiety, and the gut-brain connection. By calming the nervous system and reducing emotional triggers, hypnosis creates a healthier environment for the digestive system to function more effectively.

The Power of Belief and Expectation

One of the most significant aspects of the mind-body connection is the role of belief and expectation in shaping our physical reality. The placebo effect, where patients experience improvements in health simply because they believe they are receiving effective treatment, illustrates the power of the mind in influencing the body's responses. Hypnosis capitalizes on this concept by helping individuals reframe their beliefs about their health, pain, or healing process.

By fostering a positive mental state and encouraging self-efficacy, hypnosis helps individuals believe in their ability to heal, recover, and manage pain. This shift in mindset an trigger actual physical changes, such as reduced muscle tension, improved circulation, and the release of endorphins, all of which contribute to overall well-being.

Conclusion

The mind-body connection is a fundamental aspect of our health and well-being, with profound implications for how we manage pain, stress, and emotional challenges. Hypnosis is a powerful tool that taps into this connection, enabling individuals to access the subconscious mind and make lasting changes to both their mental and physical states. By fostering relaxation, reducing emotional distress, and promoting healing, hypnosis serves as a bridge between the mind and body, helping individuals take control of their health in a holistic way. Whether used to manage pain, heal from emotional trauma, or improve overall well-being, hypnosis illustrates the profound influence that our thoughts and beliefs have on our physical reality.

Hypnosis to Ease Physical Pain

Physical pain, whether acute or chronic, can significantly impact a person's quality of life. While traditional methods of pain management, such as medication or physical therapy, can be effective, they often come with side effects or limitations. In contrast, hypnosis offers a unique and non-invasive approach to pain relief by leveraging the power of the mind to reduce the perception of pain and promote healing. By inducing a relaxed state and guiding individuals to reframe their pain experiences, hypnosis taps into the body's natural mechanisms to alleviate discomfort.

How Hypnosis Relieves Pain

At its core, hypnosis involves entering a deeply relaxed state in which the conscious mind becomes less active, and the subconscious mind becomes more receptive to suggestions. This state of focused attention allows individuals to alter their mental and physical experiences, including their perception of pain. Hypnosis doesn't eliminate pain entirely but can significantly reduce its intensity or alter the way the brain processes the pain signals, making the discomfort more manageable.

The effectiveness of hypnosis in pain relief is rooted in its ability to influence the brain's processing of pain signals. When someone experiences pain, sensory signals are sent from the body to the brain, where they are processed and interpreted. The emotional aspect of pain, including fear or anxiety, often amplifies the sensation, making it feel more intense. Hypnosis can reduce the emotional response to pain, making it feel less overwhelming.

Mechanisms of Hypnosis in Pain Management

1. **Distraction and Focused Attention**

Hypnosis helps manage pain by redirecting the mind's focus. During a hypnotic session, individuals are guided to concentrate on a particular thought, image, or sensation that diverts attention away from the pain. For example, the hypnotist might ask the person to imagine a soothing scene, such as lying on a warm beach or walking through a peaceful forest. This focused imagery helps the brain shift away from pain signals, making the discomfort less prominent.

2. **Altering Pain Perception**

Another technique commonly used in hypnosis for pain management is changing the way pain is perceived. This might involve transforming the pain into a more tolerable form through visualization. For example, a person in pain might be instructed to imagine the sensation as a color, shape, or temperature. Once the pain is visualized in a different way, such as turning it from red-hot to a cooler blue, the brain may process the sensation as less intense. This technique, known as "cognitive restructuring," helps individuals reinterpret the physical sensation and reduces its emotional impact.

3. **Pain Modulation and Endorphin Release**

Hypnosis can also stimulate the release of endorphins, the body's natural pain-relieving chemicals. By inducing a deep state of relaxation, hypnosis activates the parasympathetic nervous system, which can trigger the production of endorphins and other neurotransmitters that contribute to pain relief. These chemicals help reduce the sensation of pain and promote a sense of well-being. The relaxation induced during hypnosis can also improve circulation and reduce muscle tension, which can further alleviate pain.

4. **Mind-Body Connection**

Pain isn't just a physical sensation; it is also a psychological experience. The way individuals think about and react to pain can influence how they feel it. When a person is anxious, stressed, or fearful, their body's response to pain is amplified, leading to greater discomfort. Hypnosis addresses this mind-body connection by promoting relaxation and reducing the emotional distress associated with pain. By calming the mind, hypnosis helps lower the body's stress response, reducing the intensity of pain.

Clinical Applications of Hypnosis for Pain Relief

Hypnosis has been successfully used in a variety of clinical settings to manage both acute and chronic pain. Research has demonstrated its effectiveness in conditions such as:

- **Chronic Pain**: Conditions like arthritis, fibromyalgia, and lower back pain often involve persistent, long-term discomfort. Hypnosis can be particularly beneficial for individuals with chronic pain, helping them reduce the intensity of their symptoms and improve their overall quality of life. Studies have shown that people with chronic pain who undergo hypnosis experience significant reductions in pain intensity and emotional distress.
- **Post-Surgical Pain**: After surgery, many patients experience pain as part of the healing process. Hypnosis has been shown to reduce post-operative pain and the need for pain medications, leading to faster recovery times and fewer complications. In one study, patients who received hypnosis as part of their post-surgery care required significantly less analgesic medication compared to those who received standard care.

- **Labor and Childbirth**: Hypnosis has long been used as a tool for pain management during labor. Through a technique called "hypnobirthing," women are trained to use deep relaxation, positive visualization, and breathing techniques to manage the pain of childbirth. Research has shown that women who use hypnosis during labor report less pain, fewer complications, and a greater sense of control during the birth process.
- **Headaches and Migraines**: Hypnosis has been found to be effective in treating tension headaches and migraines. By teaching individuals to relax and reduce muscle tension, hypnosis helps prevent the onset of headaches and can ease their severity. Research has shown that individuals with chronic headaches who use hypnosis experience fewer headaches and a reduction in the severity and duration of their pain.
- **Cancer Pain**: Pain associated with cancer can be particularly difficult to manage, and many patients turn to hypnosis as a complementary treatment. Hypnosis has been shown to reduce both the intensity of cancer-related pain and the anxiety associated with it. By promoting relaxation and reducing emotional distress, hypnosis helps individuals feel more in control of their pain and improves their overall quality of life.

Scientific Evidence Supporting Hypnosis for Pain Relief

Numerous studies support the effectiveness of hypnosis in pain management. A meta-analysis published in *The International Journal of Clinical and Experimental Hypnosis* (2000) reviewed 18 studies on hypnosis for pain management and found that hypnosis was effective in reducing pain across various conditions. The research indicated that individuals who used hypnosis experienced a significant decrease in pain intensity, anxiety, and the need for pain medications.

Another study published in *Pain Medicine* (2008) focused on the use of hypnosis for chronic pain and found that it was particularly effective for conditions like fibromyalgia and arthritis. The study participants reported significant improvements in pain levels, as well as a reduction in emotional distress related to their pain.

Advantages of Using Hypnosis for Pain Relief

One of the primary advantages of hypnosis as a pain management technique is that it is non-invasive and free from the side effects associated with many pain medications. For individuals who are sensitive to drugs or wish to avoid medications altogether, hypnosis provides a safe and effective alternative. It can also be used in conjunction with other pain management strategies to enhance their effectiveness.

Moreover, hypnosis empowers individuals to take control of their pain experience. Through self-hypnosis techniques, individuals can manage pain on their own, reducing the need for medical interventions. This sense of autonomy and control can improve emotional well-being and reduce the anxiety often associated with chronic or acute pain.

Limitations and Considerations

While hypnosis is a powerful tool for pain relief, it may not be effective for everyone. Some individuals may not be highly susceptible to hypnosis, meaning they may not experience the same level of pain reduction as others. Additionally, hypnosis is not a cure for pain conditions; rather, it is a complementary approach that works best when integrated into a comprehensive pain management plan.

Hypnosis should be used under the guidance of a trained and experienced hypnotherapist, especially for individuals dealing with complex or severe pain conditions. A trained professional can tailor the hypnosis experience to the individual's needs, ensuring that the technique is both safe and effective.

Conclusion

Hypnosis offers a promising, non-invasive approach to managing physical pain. By accessing the subconscious mind, hypnosis can alter pain perception, reduce emotional distress, and promote healing. Whether used for chronic conditions, post-surgical recovery, or acute pain relief, hypnosis provides a valuable tool in the management of pain. With its ability to empower individuals and reduce reliance on medications, hypnosis can significantly improve quality of life for those dealing with persistent discomfort.

Studies Supporting Hypnosis for Pain Management

Hypnosis has gained increasing recognition in recent decades as a powerful tool for pain management, supported by numerous studies and clinical trials. Researchers have explored its effectiveness across a wide range of conditions, from acute pain after surgery to chronic pain in conditions like arthritis and fibromyalgia. By tapping into the mind-body connection, hypnosis helps individuals manage pain by altering their perception and response to it, often reducing the need for medication and improving overall quality of life.

Clinical Evidence for Hypnosis in Acute Pain Relief

One of the most well-documented areas of hypnosis research involves its use in managing acute pain, particularly in surgical and medical settings. In a landmark study published in *The Lancet* (1994), patients undergoing surgery were divided into two groups: one that received standard pain management, and another that was treated with hypnosis as part of their care plan. The study found that those who received hypnosis required significantly less anesthesia and reported lower levels of pain during recovery. The researchers concluded that hypnosis could serve as a valuable adjunct to conventional pain management strategies, especially in reducing the need for medication.

Similarly, research conducted at the *University of Washington School of Medicine* (2006) examined the use of hypnosis in reducing post-operative pain in patients undergoing dental procedures. The study found that patients who underwent hypnosis before and during the procedure reported significantly less pain and anxiety compared to those who received traditional sedation methods. These findings suggest that hypnosis can be an effective, low-risk alternative for managing pain during and after medical procedures.

Hypnosis for Chronic Pain Conditions

Hypnosis has also proven effective in managing chronic pain, which is often more complex and resistant to traditional treatments. A review of clinical trials published in *The Journal of Pain* (2009) found that hypnosis was particularly beneficial for individuals with chronic pain conditions such as fibromyalgia, rheumatoid arthritis, and lower back pain. The study concluded that hypnosis could reduce pain intensity, improve mood, and enhance functional capacity in patients with chronic conditions. These effects

vere attributed to hypnosis's ability to alter the perception of pain and reduce the
emotional distress often associated with long-term pain.

In a 2016 study published in *The Clinical Journal of Pain*, researchers found that
hypnosis helped reduce the severity of chronic pain in individuals with fibromyalgia.
Participants who underwent hypnosis reported a significant reduction in pain levels and
experienced fewer episodes of pain flare-ups. The researchers noted that hypnosis could
be particularly helpful for managing pain in fibromyalgia patients, as it targets both the
sensory and emotional components of the pain experience.

Pain Reduction in Cancer Patients

Cancer-related pain presents a unique challenge, as it often involves not only physical
discomfort but also emotional distress and anxiety. Numerous studies have explored the
role of hypnosis in alleviating cancer pain, with promising results. A study published in
Cancer (2007) focused on patients receiving chemotherapy and found that those who
participated in a hypnosis program experienced less pain, nausea, and fatigue compared
to those who did not. The study participants also reported an improved sense of well-
being and greater control over their pain, highlighting hypnosis's potential as a
complementary therapy for cancer patients.

In another study published in *The Journal of Clinical Oncology* (2010), researchers
examined the use of hypnosis in managing pain in cancer patients who were experiencing
advanced-stage disease. The results indicated that hypnosis not only reduced pain
intensity but also improved the patients' ability to cope with the emotional and
psychological aspects of their illness. This is particularly significant, as many cancer
patients experience psychological distress that exacerbates their physical pain, making
hypnosis a valuable tool in providing holistic care.

The Role of Hypnosis in Headache and Migraines

Headaches, including chronic tension headaches and migraines, are common conditions
that significantly impact daily life. Several studies have demonstrated that hypnosis can
be effective in reducing the frequency and severity of these conditions. A 2007 study
published in *Headache: The Journal of Head and Face Pain* found that individuals who
underwent hypnosis experienced fewer and less intense migraine episodes compared to
those who received standard treatment. The study's authors noted that hypnosis might
alter the brain's pain processing pathways, leading to a reduction in migraine-related
discomfort.

A 2010 meta-analysis published in *The International Journal of Clinical and
Experimental Hypnosis* reviewed multiple studies on hypnosis for headache management.
The analysis found that hypnosis significantly reduced both the frequency and severity of
headaches in participants, and that these effects were sustained over time. The researchers

concluded that hypnosis could be a highly effective and cost-efficient treatment for individuals with chronic headaches, particularly those who have not responded well to medication.

Chronic pain is often exacerbated by emotional and psychological stress, making the mind-body connection a key focus in pain management. Research has shown that hypnosis can be particularly beneficial for conditions where stress plays a major role, such as irritable bowel syndrome (IBS), temporomandibular joint disorders (TMJ), and fibromyalgia. A study published in *The American Journal of Clinical Hypnosis* (2010) examined the use of hypnosis in IBS patients and found that hypnosis led to a significant reduction in abdominal pain, bloating, and discomfort. The study also noted that patients who received hypnosis experienced a reduction in stress levels, further supporting the role of hypnosis in managing pain through emotional regulation.

For individuals with TMJ, a condition often linked to jaw pain and muscle tension, hypnosis has been shown to reduce both pain and stress. A 2009 study published in *The Journal of the American Dental Association* found that hypnosis, in combination with traditional dental care, led to significant reductions in pain and jaw discomfort in patients with TMJ. The study emphasized that hypnosis's ability to promote relaxation and alleviate stress played a crucial role in managing this often painful condition.

Hypnosis for Acute Pain in Children

Hypnosis has also shown promise in managing acute pain in pediatric patients. A study published in *Pediatric Anesthesia* (2005) examined the use of hypnosis in children undergoing minor medical procedures, such as needle injections and wound care. The researchers found that children who received hypnosis experienced less pain and anxiety compared to those who were treated with standard methods. In addition, the children who underwent hypnosis were less likely to require sedatives or pain medications, demonstrating the potential of hypnosis as a safe, effective alternative for managing acute pain in children.

The Mechanisms Behind Hypnosis in Pain Management

The underlying mechanisms of hypnosis in pain management are still being explored, but several theories suggest how hypnosis may work. One key mechanism is the modulation of pain perception through changes in the brain's pain-processing centers. Neuroimaging studies have shown that hypnosis can alter brain activity in areas associated with sensory processing and pain perception, suggesting that hypnosis influences the way pain signals are processed and interpreted by the brain.

Additionally, hypnosis may reduce the emotional and psychological factors that amplify pain. By promoting deep relaxation and reducing anxiety, hypnosis helps lower the body's stress response, which can exacerbate pain. The reduction in stress hormones such as cortisol can lead to improved pain tolerance and an overall sense of well-being.

Conclusion

The growing body of research supporting hypnosis as an effective tool for pain management highlights its potential to alleviate both acute and chronic pain. Studies have demonstrated its benefits in a variety of conditions, from post-surgical recovery to chronic pain syndromes like fibromyalgia, cancer pain, and headaches. By harnessing the mind-body connection, hypnosis can alter pain perception, reduce emotional distress, and promote relaxation, offering a valuable adjunct to traditional pain management methods. As more research is conducted, hypnosis's role in pain relief is likely to expand, providing individuals with a safe, non-invasive alternative to manage pain and improve their quality of life.

Hypnosis for Behavioral Change

Hypnosis has long been recognized as a powerful tool for influencing behavior, helping individuals modify unwanted habits, adopt healthier lifestyle choices, and overcome psychological barriers. By accessing the subconscious mind, hypnosis allows individuals to bypass the critical filters of the conscious mind, making it easier to instill new behaviors and attitudes that align with their goals. This ability to facilitate behavioral change has made hypnosis a popular choice for addressing a wide range of issues, from smoking cessation to weight loss, and even improving performance in areas like sports and public speaking.

How Hypnosis Facilitates Behavioral Change

At its core, hypnosis works by inducing a relaxed state that allows a person to enter a heightened state of suggestibility. This doesn't mean that a person loses control or is made to do something against their will, as is often depicted in movies. Rather, it means that the conscious mind becomes less active, and the subconscious mind becomes more receptive to positive suggestions. The subconscious mind plays a significant role in shaping behavior, as it holds beliefs, patterns, and habits formed over a lifetime. By targeting these subconscious patterns, hypnosis helps individuals reframe their thinking and replace negative behaviors with more constructive ones.

In this relaxed state, a trained hypnotherapist can offer suggestions that aim to influence thought patterns and behavior. For example, someone who struggles with overeating might be guided to imagine themselves feeling full after eating smaller portions, or to envision healthy foods as more appealing than unhealthy options. These suggestions, when reinforced through multiple sessions, can create lasting changes in how the individual responds to certain triggers, ultimately leading to the desired behavioral changes.

Hypnosis for Breaking Unwanted Habits

One of the most common uses of hypnosis is for breaking unwanted habits. Whether it's smoking, nail-biting, or excessive drinking, these habits often become deeply ingrained in the subconscious mind, making them difficult to overcome with sheer willpower alone. Hypnosis offers a unique way to address the root causes of these habits by helping individuals reprogram their subconscious beliefs and associations.

For example, hypnosis has been widely used to help individuals quit smoking. A person's desire to smoke is often linked to subconscious cues such as stress, boredom, or social situations. Through hypnosis, individuals can be guided to associate these triggers with more positive behaviors, such as taking a deep breath or drinking water instead of reaching for a cigarette. Additionally, hypnosis can help individuals visualize themselves as non-smokers, reinforcing the idea that they can live a life free from nicotine addiction.

Similarly, hypnosis can be used to break other habits, like overindulgence in food, procrastination, or excessive drinking. By addressing the subconscious causes of these behaviors and replacing them with healthier responses, hypnosis can facilitate lasting behavioral change without the need for harsh willpower or restrictive approaches.

Weight Loss and Healthy Eating Habits

Weight loss is another area where hypnosis has shown promising results. Traditional weight loss methods, such as dieting and exercising, can be effective, but they often fail when individuals struggle with emotional eating or psychological barriers to change. Hypnosis can address these underlying issues by helping individuals develop a healthier relationship with food and their bodies.

In a typical hypnosis session for weight loss, a hypnotherapist may guide the individual to visualize their ideal weight or size and create a mental image of themselves enjoying healthier foods while feeling satisfied with smaller portions. This positive reinforcement helps the individual change their mindset around food and eating. Additionally, hypnosis can be used to address emotional triggers for overeating, such as stress, anxiety, or boredom. By altering the subconscious associations with food, hypnosis can make it easier to adopt healthier eating habits and stick to a sustainable weight loss plan.

Improving Self-Confidence and Motivation

Hypnosis is also commonly used to enhance self-confidence and motivation, which are crucial elements for achieving behavioral change. Individuals often struggle to make lasting changes because they lack belief in their ability to succeed or feel overwhelmed by the task ahead. Hypnosis can help by boosting self-esteem and reinforcing the individual's sense of capability and resilience.

For example, someone preparing for a public speaking engagement may struggle with nerves and self-doubt. Through hypnosis, the individual can be guided to visualize themselves speaking confidently in front of an audience, with a calm and clear mind. This positive mental imagery can build self-confidence and reduce anxiety. Over time, with repeated suggestions and reinforcement, the individual may feel more comfortable in social situations and more motivated to pursue their goals.

Similarly, hypnosis has been used to help athletes enhance performance by improving focus, motivation, and mental clarity. Through visualization techniques, athletes can mentally rehearse their performance, overcoming doubts and building a stronger belief in their abilities. This psychological preparation can improve outcomes in everything from competitive sports to everyday tasks.

Hypnosis for Stress Management and Emotional Well-being

Behavioral change is often tied to emotional and psychological well-being, and hypnosis is particularly effective in managing stress and emotional challenges. Stress and anxiety can trigger negative behaviors like overeating, smoking, or drinking, which in turn contribute to poor health and reduced quality of life. Hypnosis offers a powerful tool for addressing these emotional issues by promoting relaxation and emotional balance.

Hypnotherapy can help individuals develop healthier coping mechanisms for stress, replacing reactive behaviors with more constructive responses. For example, individuals may be taught to relax and breathe deeply when they feel stressed, or to use mental imagery to reduce anxiety. Hypnosis also helps individuals reframe negative thought patterns, replacing feelings of inadequacy or self-doubt with more empowering beliefs. This transformation can create lasting change in behavior by addressing the root causes of stress and emotional distress.

Scientific Evidence Supporting Hypnosis for Behavioral Change

There is growing evidence supporting the effectiveness of hypnosis for behavior modification. Studies have shown that hypnosis can significantly improve outcomes in areas such as smoking cessation, weight loss, and stress management.

A meta-analysis published in *The Journal of Consulting and Clinical Psychology* (2000) reviewed the effectiveness of hypnosis in smoking cessation. The analysis found that individuals who used hypnosis to quit smoking were more likely to remain smoke-free compared to those who used other methods, such as nicotine replacement therapy or willpower alone. The study concluded that hypnosis can be an effective intervention for smoking cessation, especially when combined with other behavioral treatments.

Similarly, a study published in *Obesity Reviews* (2015) examined the use of hypnosis in weight loss programs. The research found that hypnosis, when combined with cognitive-behavioral therapy, significantly improved weight loss outcomes and helped individuals maintain their weight loss over time. Hypnosis was particularly effective in addressing emotional eating and other psychological barriers to weight loss.

In the realm of stress management, research has shown that hypnosis can reduce symptoms of anxiety, depression, and post-traumatic stress disorder (PTSD). A 2016 study published in *The American Journal of Clinical Hypnosis* found that individuals who underwent hypnosis reported significant reductions in stress and anxiety levels, as well as improvements in overall emotional well-being.

Conclusion

Hypnosis offers a powerful and effective method for achieving behavioral change, from breaking unwanted habits to improving self-confidence and managing stress. By accessing the subconscious mind, hypnosis allows individuals to reprogram limiting beliefs and behaviors, replacing them with more positive, goal-oriented actions. Whether used to quit smoking, lose weight, or overcome emotional challenges, hypnosis can be a transformative tool in creating lasting changes in behavior. As research continues to support its efficacy, hypnosis is likely to become an increasingly popular option for individuals seeking to improve their lives through the power of their own minds.

Smoking and Hypnosis

For many individuals, smoking is not just a physical habit but a deeply ingrained psychological pattern. Breaking free from smoking often requires more than just willpower—it involves addressing the subconscious triggers that drive the behavior. Hypnosis offers a powerful approach to smoking cessation by working directly with the subconscious mind, helping individuals reframe their associations with smoking and break free from nicotine addiction.

How Hypnosis Works for Smoking Cessation

Hypnosis works by inducing a relaxed, focused state in which the mind becomes more receptive to positive suggestions. When a person is in this state, the critical conscious mind is less active, allowing the therapist to communicate directly with the subconscious. In the case of smoking, the hypnotherapist helps the individual identify and alter the subconscious cues that prompt the desire to smoke. These triggers may include stress, social situations, or even boredom.

Through guided suggestions, the individual may be encouraged to visualize themselves a a non-smoker or to associate the act of smoking with unpleasant sensations or consequences. For example, hypnosis can help a smoker reframe their desire for a cigarette by associating it with feelings of disgust or unease, thereby reducing the emotional appeal of the habit. Over time, these suggestions can lead to lasting behavioral change, making it easier for the individual to resist the urge to smoke.

Breaking the Psychological Addiction

One of the most powerful aspects of smoking addiction is its psychological component. Many smokers are deeply attached to the idea of smoking as a way to relax, cope with stress, or take breaks throughout the day. These associations are often deeply rooted in the subconscious mind and are reinforced over time. Hypnosis works to break these associations by changing how the individual perceives smoking.

For example, hypnosis can help individuals reframe smoking as a harmful, unnecessary activity rather than a pleasurable or relaxing one. It may also address emotional triggers, helping the individual develop healthier coping mechanisms for stress or anxiety. By shifting the subconscious mindset, hypnosis makes it easier for individuals to embrace a non-smoking identity and replace old patterns with new, healthier behaviors.

Research and Effectiveness of Hypnosis for Smoking Cessation

There is growing evidence supporting the effectiveness of hypnosis in helping people quit smoking. In a meta-analysis published in *The Journal of Consulting and Clinical Psychology* (2000), researchers reviewed 59 studies on smoking cessation treatments and found that hypnosis was significantly more effective than other methods, such as willpower alone or behavioral counseling. The analysis concluded that hypnosis, particularly when combined with other therapeutic techniques, increased the chances of quitting smoking and remaining smoke-free.

In another study published in *The American Journal of Clinical Hypnosis* (2005), researchers examined the long-term effects of hypnosis on smoking cessation. The study found that individuals who underwent hypnosis were more likely to remain smoke-free for at least six months compared to those who used other methods, such as nicotine replacement therapy. These findings suggest that hypnosis may offer lasting benefits for individuals seeking to quit smoking.

The Role of Suggestion in Hypnosis for Smoking

The success of hypnosis in smoking cessation often hinges on the quality of the suggestions given during the session. Hypnotherapists tailor their suggestions to the individual's specific triggers and needs. For example, a smoker who tends to light up when feeling stressed may be guided to visualize themselves managing stress in healthier ways, such as through deep breathing or meditation. On the other hand, a smoker who associates cigarettes with social situations may be encouraged to feel confident and comfortable in those situations without needing a cigarette.

The effectiveness of hypnosis relies on both the skill of the therapist and the willingness of the individual to engage in the process. While some people may respond to hypnosis after just one session, others may require multiple sessions to reinforce the suggestions and ensure long-term success. Regardless of the number of sessions required, the goal is to shift the individual's subconscious belief system, making smoking no longer appealing or desirable.

Additional Benefits of Hypnosis for Smokers

In addition to helping individuals quit smoking, hypnosis can also address the underlying issues that often accompany smoking addiction. Many smokers turn to cigarettes as a way to manage stress, anxiety, or emotional discomfort. Hypnosis can help individuals develop healthier coping strategies, such as relaxation techniques or mindfulness practices, which can be used as alternatives to smoking.

Furthermore, hypnosis can reduce the withdrawal symptoms associated with quitting smoking. Nicotine withdrawal often leads to irritability, cravings, and difficulty concentrating. Hypnosis helps by calming the nervous system and promoting relaxation, making the process of quitting less stressful and more manageable.

Limitations and Considerations

While hypnosis can be highly effective for smoking cessation, it is not a guaranteed solution for everyone. The success of hypnosis depends on several factors, including the individual's level of commitment to quitting, their susceptibility to hypnosis, and the skill of the hypnotherapist. Additionally, hypnosis may not be as effective for individuals who have deep psychological or emotional issues related to their smoking habit, such as severe anxiety or trauma.

It is also important to note that hypnosis is often most effective when combined with other smoking cessation strategies. For instance, individuals may benefit from a comprehensive approach that includes behavioral therapy, nicotine replacement therapy, or support groups, in addition to hypnotherapy.

Conclusion

Hypnosis offers a promising and effective method for quitting smoking by addressing both the psychological and behavioral aspects of the addiction. By accessing the subconscious mind and changing the associations, triggers, and beliefs that drive smoking, hypnosis helps individuals break free from the cycle of nicotine dependence. Supported by growing research and clinical evidence, hypnosis can be a valuable tool for those looking to quit smoking and embrace a healthier, smoke-free lifestyle. Whether used as a standalone treatment or as part of a broader cessation plan, hypnosis empowers individuals to take control of their health and overcome the powerful grip of smoking addiction.

Weight Loss and Hypnosis

For many individuals struggling with weight loss, the journey often feels like an endless battle against cravings, emotional triggers, and deeply ingrained eating habits. While traditional methods like dieting and exercise can be effective, they may not address the underlying psychological factors that contribute to overeating or poor food choices. Hypnosis offers a unique solution by targeting the subconscious mind, helping individuals make lasting changes to their relationship with food, appetite, and body image.

How Hypnosis Supports Weight Loss

Hypnosis works by inducing a deeply relaxed state in which the conscious mind becomes less active, allowing the subconscious mind to become more receptive to positive suggestions. This altered state of awareness creates an opportunity to reprogram subconscious thoughts, beliefs, and habits that contribute to unhealthy eating patterns. Unlike traditional weight loss methods, which focus primarily on physical changes, hypnosis targets the mental and emotional factors that drive overeating, such as stress, boredom, emotional eating, and low self-esteem.

Through hypnosis, individuals can be guided to reframe their thoughts and behaviors around food. For example, they might begin to associate healthy foods with positive feelings of satisfaction, energy, and vitality, while linking unhealthy foods to negative associations like discomfort or guilt. These mental shifts can make it easier to make healthier food choices without feeling deprived or restricted.

Addressing Emotional Eating

One of the key benefits of hypnosis for weight loss is its ability to address emotional eating. Many people use food as a way to cope with stress, anxiety, boredom, or negative emotions. These emotional triggers can lead to overeating or eating unhealthy comfort foods, which can sabotage weight loss efforts. Hypnosis can help break this cycle by teaching individuals to identify and manage emotional triggers without turning to food.

In a typical hypnosis session for emotional eating, the hypnotherapist may guide the individual to visualize themselves dealing with stress or emotions in healthier ways— such as through relaxation, mindfulness, or physical activity—rather than relying on food for comfort. Over time, these new responses can become automatic, reducing the urge to eat emotionally and promoting healthier coping strategies.

Changing Habits and Behaviors

Hypnosis can also help individuals change deeply ingrained habits that contribute to weight gain, such as mindless snacking, overeating at mealtimes, or emotional cravings for sugary or fatty foods. By accessing the subconscious mind, hypnosis can help individuals modify these behaviors at their core, making it easier to adopt healthier habits.

For example, hypnosis can encourage individuals to visualize themselves feeling full and satisfied after smaller portions, or to feel a sense of enjoyment and satisfaction from healthy foods like vegetables, fruits, and lean proteins. These positive associations can gradually replace the old habit of overeating or choosing unhealthy foods, making it easier to stick to a balanced, nutritious diet.

Visualization and Motivation

In addition to changing eating behaviors, hypnosis can be used to increase motivation and self-confidence in the weight loss process. Many individuals struggle with feelings of discouragement or self-doubt during their weight loss journey, especially if they've experienced setbacks or failed attempts in the past. Hypnosis can help boost self-esteem and reinforce the belief that weight loss is achievable and sustainable.

Through guided visualization techniques, individuals can imagine themselves achieving their weight loss goals and enjoying the benefits of a healthier body and lifestyle. These visualizations can create a sense of excitement and determination, helping individuals stay focused and motivated to continue their efforts. Visualization also strengthens the mind-body connection, encouraging individuals to adopt a positive mindset and feel empowered to make the changes necessary to achieve their goals.

Research on Hypnosis for Weight Loss

Several studies have explored the effectiveness of hypnosis in weight loss, with promising results. In a meta-analysis published in *The International Journal of Clinical and Experimental Hypnosis* (2014), researchers found that individuals who underwent hypnotherapy for weight loss were significantly more likely to lose weight and maintain their weight loss over time compared to those who relied on traditional weight loss methods alone. The study concluded that hypnosis could enhance the results of conventional weight loss programs by addressing the psychological factors that contribute to overeating and poor food choices.

Another study, published in *The American Journal of Clinical Hypnosis* (2015), investigated the long-term effects of hypnosis on weight loss. The results showed that individuals who combined hypnosis with other behavioral therapies achieved more significant weight loss and were better able to maintain their results over a six-month period. These findings suggest that hypnosis can be an effective tool not only for initiating weight loss but also for ensuring long-term success.

Hypnosis for Healthy Lifestyle Changes

While hypnosis is often associated with weight loss, it can also help individuals adopt a healthier overall lifestyle. In addition to promoting better eating habits, hypnosis can encourage regular physical activity, improve sleep quality, and reduce stress—all of which play a crucial role in maintaining a healthy weight. By helping individuals shift their mindset to one of self-care and well-being, hypnosis can create lasting lifestyle changes that support long-term health and weight management.

For example, individuals who struggle with finding the motivation to exercise may be guided to visualize themselves enjoying physical activity, feeling energized and motivated to move their bodies. Hypnosis can also help reduce stress levels, which can be a major barrier to weight loss, by promoting relaxation and healthy coping strategies. As individuals make healthier choices in all areas of their lives, they are more likely to achieve and maintain their desired weight.

Is Hypnosis Right for You?

While hypnosis can be a highly effective tool for weight loss, it is important to note that it is not a quick fix or a substitute for healthy lifestyle changes. For best results, hypnosis should be used as part of a comprehensive weight loss plan that includes a balanced diet, regular physical activity, and emotional support. Additionally, individuals must be open to the process and willing to engage with the suggestions and visualizations provided during hypnosis sessions.

It is also important to seek a qualified hypnotherapist who is trained in weight loss and behavioral change. A skilled professional can help tailor the sessions to your specific needs and goals, ensuring that the hypnosis process is both effective and empowering.

Conclusion

Hypnosis offers a unique and powerful approach to weight loss by addressing the psychological factors that contribute to unhealthy eating habits and emotional eating. By reprogramming the subconscious mind, hypnosis helps individuals make lasting changes to their behaviors, perceptions, and relationships with food. Whether used to break emotional eating patterns, enhance motivation, or support a healthy lifestyle, hypnosis can be a valuable tool for anyone seeking to achieve long-term weight loss success.

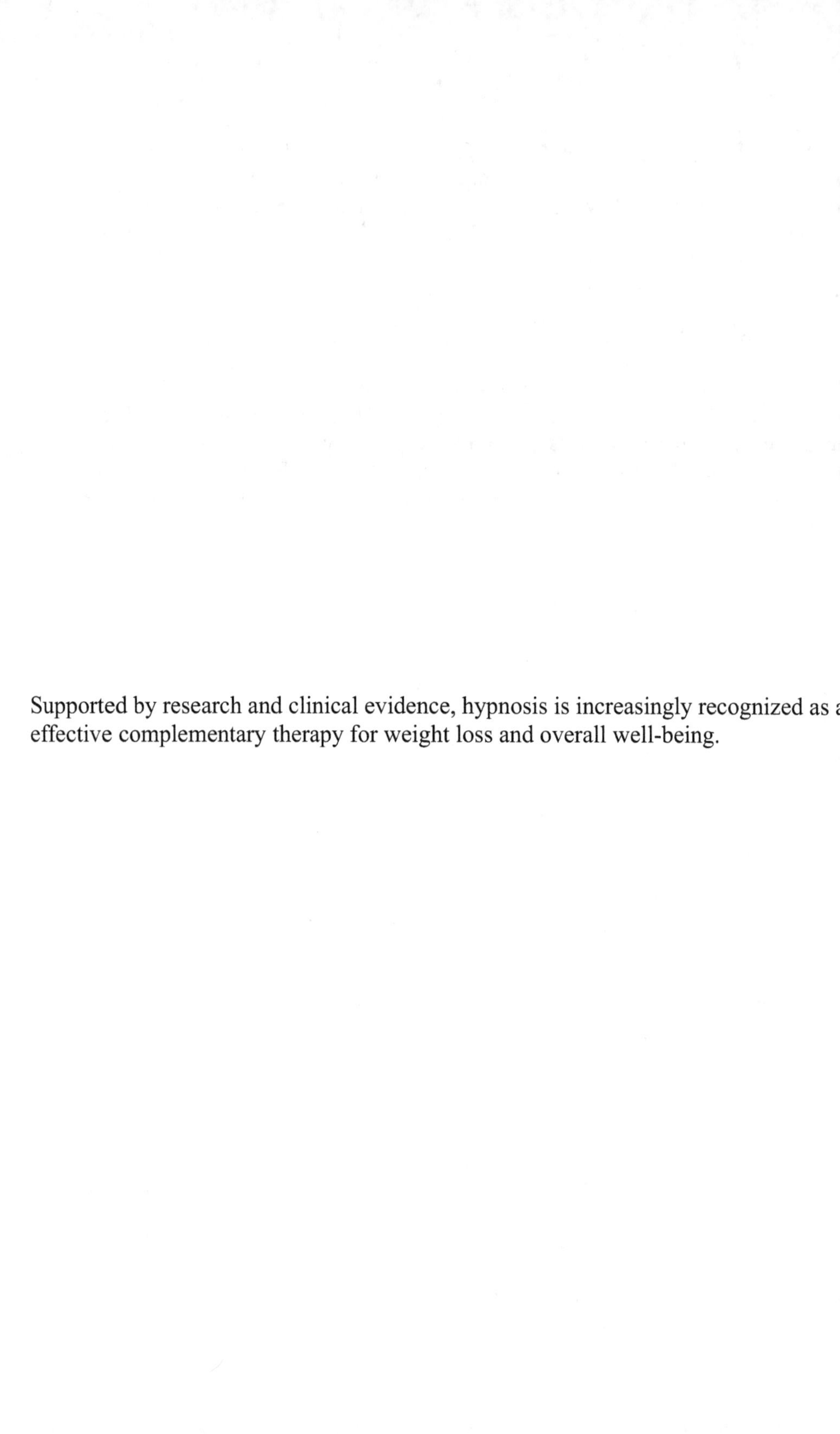

Supported by research and clinical evidence, hypnosis is increasingly recognized as an effective complementary therapy for weight loss and overall well-being.

Other Habits That Can Be Changed with Hypnosis

Hypnosis is a powerful tool for transforming unwanted behaviors and habits by accessing the subconscious mind. While it is often associated with smoking cessation and weight loss, hypnosis can be used to address a wide range of habits, behaviors, and mental patterns that are ingrained at a subconscious level. By inducing a state of focused relaxation, hypnosis allows individuals to bypass their critical conscious mind and directly influence the underlying psychological processes that contribute to habitual actions.

Overcoming Nail Biting

Nail biting is a common habit that many individuals struggle to break, often due to anxiety, stress, or simply out of habit. Through hypnosis, the subconscious mind can be retrained to view nail biting as an undesirable behavior. The process involves identifying the underlying triggers—whether they are related to stress, boredom, or anxiety—and replacing the urge with healthier alternatives, such as relaxation techniques or tapping into positive visualizations. As the individual becomes more relaxed and confident in managing stress or anxiety, the desire to bite nails diminishes.

Reducing Procrastination

Procrastination is another habit that can be tackled effectively through hypnosis. Often, procrastination stems from deeper psychological issues such as fear of failure, perfectionism, or lack of motivation. Hypnosis works by helping individuals uncover the root cause of their procrastination and reprogramming the subconscious mind to overcome these barriers. Suggestions can be made to enhance motivation, boost productivity, and foster a more positive attitude toward tasks. By addressing the deeper emotional and psychological factors that contribute to procrastination, hypnosis enables individuals to adopt more productive habits and create a stronger sense of personal responsibility.

Overcoming Fears and Phobias

Hypnosis is widely known for its ability to help individuals overcome irrational fears and phobias, such as fear of flying, spiders, or public speaking. Phobias are often rooted in past experiences or subconscious beliefs that cause the individual to respond with intense fear or anxiety. In hypnosis, the therapist helps the individual access these subconscious memories or beliefs and works to replace them with more rational and calming thoughts. Through repeated sessions, the subconscious mind can be conditioned to respond with calmness rather than fear, helping individuals face situations that once seemed overwhelming.

Improving Sleep Patterns

Many individuals struggle with sleep disorders such as insomnia, restless sleep, or difficulty falling asleep due to stress, anxiety, or overactive thinking. Hypnosis can be highly effective in promoting better sleep by helping individuals relax deeply and clear their minds before bedtime. Through guided relaxation techniques and visualizations, hypnosis helps to reprogram the subconscious mind to associate sleep with calmness, comfort, and peace. Over time, individuals can achieve a more consistent and restful sleep pattern, leading to improved overall health and well-being.

Enhancing Self-Confidence and Self-Esteem

Low self-confidence and self-esteem can hold individuals back from reaching their potential in various aspects of life, including career, relationships, and personal growth. Hypnosis can help by addressing the negative self-beliefs that are often deeply embedded in the subconscious. By accessing the subconscious mind, a trained hypnotherapist can help the individual replace limiting beliefs with empowering thoughts, improving their self-image and boosting confidence. Hypnosis can also reinforce positive affirmations, helping the individual adopt a more positive outlook on themselves and their abilities.

Managing Anger and Frustration

Anger issues are often rooted in deep-seated emotional responses that can lead to destructive behaviors. Hypnosis can help individuals identify the triggers for their anger, whether they are past experiences, unresolved conflicts, or stress. In a hypnotic state, individuals are guided to release pent-up frustration and reframe their emotional responses. Hypnotherapy helps change the subconscious patterns that lead to explosive or irrational anger, replacing them with more controlled, calm responses. This enables individuals to manage anger in a healthier way, improving relationships and emotional well-being.

Breaking Addictive Behaviors

Addictive behaviors, whether related to substance abuse, gambling, or compulsive behaviors like shopping or overeating, can be difficult to break without addressing the psychological triggers that fuel the addiction. Hypnosis works by helping individuals access the subconscious patterns that support addictive behavior. By replacing these patterns with healthier coping mechanisms and reinforcing positive changes, hypnosis can be a powerful tool for addiction recovery. The therapy often involves strengthening the individual's sense of self-control, enhancing their ability to resist urges, and fostering a sense of empowerment.

Improving Public Speaking Skills

Fear of public speaking, also known as glossophobia, affects many people and can hinder professional and personal growth. Hypnosis can help reduce the anxiety and fear associated with public speaking by addressing subconscious beliefs about self-worth and performance. Through positive suggestions and visualizations, hypnosis helps individuals reframe their thoughts about public speaking, replacing fear with confidence. Hypnotherapy can also help individuals become more relaxed in front of an audience, improving their ability to communicate effectively and with ease.

Enhancing Sports Performance

Athletes have long used hypnosis to improve their performance, whether by enhancing focus, reducing performance anxiety, or overcoming mental barriers. Hypnosis can help athletes visualize success, boost confidence, and focus on their goals. It allows athletes to tap into their subconscious mind, reinforcing positive beliefs about their skills and abilities. By focusing on mental imagery and relaxation techniques, hypnosis helps athletes stay calm and focused under pressure, resulting in improved performance and consistency.

Managing Chronic Pain

Chronic pain, whether from conditions like arthritis, fibromyalgia, or migraines, can be debilitating and difficult to manage. Hypnosis can be an effective complementary treatment for pain management by helping individuals alter their perception of pain. Through techniques such as dissociation (mentally separating the feeling of pain from the body) or guided imagery (visualizing the pain as something manageable), hypnosis can help reduce the intensity of chronic pain. By addressing both the physical and emotional components of pain, hypnosis can provide relief and improve quality of life.

Conclusion

Hypnosis is a versatile tool that can help individuals change a wide variety of habits and behaviors that are deeply rooted in the subconscious mind. Whether it's breaking free from addiction, overcoming fears, managing stress, or improving performance, hypnosis offers a safe and effective way to create lasting change. By reprogramming the subconscious mind, individuals can develop healthier habits, improve their mental well-being, and achieve personal goals they may have once thought unattainable. Whether used as a standalone therapy or as a complement to other approaches, hypnosis is an empowering tool for transformation.

Self-Hypnosis

Self-hypnosis is a powerful tool that allows individuals to harness the benefits of hypnosis without needing a professional hypnotherapist. It involves entering a relaxed, focused state of mind where the conscious mind becomes less dominant, and the subconscious is more open to suggestion. While traditionally guided by a trained hypnotist, self-hypnosis enables individuals to create positive changes in their thoughts, behaviors, and emotions, all through their own efforts.

How Self-Hypnosis Works

Self-hypnosis is based on the same principles as professional hypnosis. When a person enters a hypnotic state, they experience deep relaxation, focused attention, and heightened awareness. In this state, the conscious mind steps back, and the subconscious mind becomes more receptive to positive suggestions or affirmations.

The process typically involves finding a quiet and comfortable space, focusing on the breath or an object, and then using specific techniques to deepen the relaxation. Once deeply relaxed, individuals can begin to offer themselves positive suggestions or visualize the desired changes they wish to make. These suggestions are aimed at shifting subconscious beliefs or creating new habits.

Techniques for Self-Hypnosis

There are several techniques that can be used to induce self-hypnosis, and different methods work better for different people. Some of the most common techniques include:

1. **Progressive Relaxation**: This method involves relaxing the body progressively, starting from the toes and working upwards toward the head. By focusing on each muscle group and consciously relaxing it, the body reaches a state of deep relaxation, which helps prepare the mind for hypnosis.
2. **Breathing Techniques**: Slow, deep, and controlled breathing can be a powerful tool for inducing relaxation. By focusing on the breath, individuals can calm their nervous system, lower stress levels, and enter a more suggestible state.
3. **Visualization**: Visualization involves imagining a peaceful scene or a goal that you wish to achieve. This can help calm the mind and direct your subconscious to focus on positive outcomes. For example, visualizing yourself successfully

overcoming an obstacle or feeling more confident can create mental shifts that support these changes in your waking life.

4. **Affirmations and Suggestions**: Once deeply relaxed, individuals can use positive affirmations and suggestions to guide the subconscious mind toward a desired change. For instance, if the goal is to quit smoking, one might repeat, "I am a non-smoker," or "I no longer crave cigarettes." Repeatedly suggesting these positive changes can help embed them into the subconscious.

5. **Counting Down**: Another common method to enter a hypnotic state involves counting down slowly from 10 to 1 while mentally relaxing and focusing on each number. With each number, the mind and body relax further, creating a deeper state of focus and relaxation.

6. **Eye Fixation**: Some individuals use an object to focus their attention, such as a candle or a spot on the wall. Staring at the object while allowing the mind to become more focused and relaxed can help induce a trance-like state.

Benefits of Self-Hypnosis

Self-hypnosis offers numerous benefits, both psychological and physical. Some of the key advantages include:

1. **Stress and Anxiety Reduction**: One of the most common uses for self-hypnosis is to reduce stress and anxiety. The deep relaxation that accompanies the process can help lower cortisol levels, calm the nervous system, and induce a feeling of peace and well-being. This makes self-hypnosis an effective tool for managing everyday stressors or acute anxiety.

2. **Improved Sleep**: Many individuals struggle with insomnia or disrupted sleep patterns. Self-hypnosis can promote restful sleep by calming the mind, reducing racing thoughts, and fostering relaxation before bedtime. Through regular practice individuals may develop new sleep habits that improve their overall sleep quality.

3. **Pain Management**: Self-hypnosis is also commonly used for pain relief. By focusing on relaxation and using mental techniques to alter the perception of pain, individuals can reduce discomfort from chronic pain, headaches, or acute injuries. Studies have shown that self-hypnosis can be effective in lowering pain intensity and improving pain tolerance.

4. **Behavioral Change**: Self-hypnosis can be a powerful tool for changing unwanted habits and behaviors. Whether it's quitting smoking, reducing overeating, or overcoming a phobia, self-hypnosis can reprogram the subconscious mind to adopt healthier behaviors and beliefs. With consistent practice, individuals can change long-standing patterns and create lasting positive transformations.

5. **Increased Confidence and Self-Esteem**: By using self-hypnosis to reinforce positive affirmations and beliefs, individuals can build greater self-confidence and improve their self-esteem. Hypnosis allows people to access the deeper parts of

their minds where limiting beliefs may have taken root and replace them with empowering thoughts that align with their goals and self-worth.

6. **Improved Focus and Concentration**: Self-hypnosis can also be used to improve focus and concentration, especially for individuals who struggle with attention or mental clarity. Through visualization techniques and mental conditioning, people can train their minds to stay focused on specific tasks, improving productivity and cognitive performance.

Is Self-Hypnosis Effective?

Research supports the effectiveness of self-hypnosis for a variety of conditions, including pain management, stress reduction, and behavior modification. While it's not a magical solution or a quick fix, when practiced consistently, self-hypnosis can produce lasting results. The key to success is repetition and dedication—by practicing regularly, the subconscious mind can be retrained to adopt new, healthier patterns of thinking and behavior.

That being said, self-hypnosis may not be suitable for everyone. Individuals with deep-rooted psychological conditions or those who have difficulty entering a relaxed state might benefit from guidance from a trained hypnotherapist. A hypnotherapist can help individuals develop the skills and techniques necessary for successful self-hypnosis and address more complex issues.

Getting Started with Self-Hypnosis

To begin practicing self-hypnosis, it's important to create an environment conducive to relaxation. This means finding a quiet, comfortable space where distractions are minimized. With regular practice, individuals can gradually improve their ability to enter a relaxed state and use self-hypnosis effectively to address their specific goals.

For those new to self-hypnosis, it can be helpful to start with guided hypnosis recordings, which provide step-by-step instructions and voice prompts to assist in the process. As individuals become more familiar with the techniques, they can gradually rely less on external guidance and develop the ability to practice self-hypnosis on their own.

Conclusion

Self-hypnosis is a valuable and accessible tool that allows individuals to tap into the power of the subconscious mind to promote positive changes. Whether for stress relief, improving sleep, managing pain, or changing behaviors, self-hypnosis can be an effective and empowering technique. By incorporating self-hypnosis into their daily routine, individuals can improve their mental and physical well-being, enhance their confidence, and create lasting, positive transformations in their lives.

Understanding Self-Hypnosis

Self-hypnosis is a practice that allows individuals to enter a focused, relaxed state of mind in order to make positive changes in their thoughts, behaviors, and emotional responses. This state, often referred to as a trance, is one where the subconscious mind becomes highly receptive to suggestion, allowing for deep relaxation and mental shifts. While often associated with therapeutic use, self-hypnosis can be a valuable tool for anyone looking to manage stress, break bad habits, enhance performance, or improve overall well-being.

The Mechanism Behind Self-Hypnosis

At its core, self-hypnosis is a process of guiding the mind into a relaxed, highly focused state. In this state, the conscious mind—the part of us that is analytical, judgmental, and critical—becomes less dominant. As the conscious mind relaxes, the subconscious mind takes center stage, becoming more open to suggestions. The process often involves using techniques such as focused attention, deep breathing, and progressive relaxation to ease the body and mind into a receptive state.

When a person is in this state, they are not asleep or unconscious, but rather in a heightened state of awareness and concentration. This allows them to bypass the usual mental filters and limiting beliefs that may prevent change in their waking life.

How to Induce Self-Hypnosis

Inducing self-hypnosis requires practice, but it can be learned by anyone willing to commit to the process. There are several techniques that are commonly used to enter a trance-like state:

1. **Progressive Relaxation**: This involves systematically relaxing each part of the body, starting from the feet and working upwards to the head. As the muscles relax, the mind follows suit, entering a deeper state of calm and focus.
2. **Breathing Techniques**: Slow, deep, and controlled breathing is a key component of self-hypnosis. By focusing on the breath and practicing slow inhales and exhales, the body's nervous system is calmed, which helps to facilitate relaxation.
3. **Visualization**: Using vivid mental imagery is a powerful tool for self-hypnosis. Visualizing peaceful and relaxing scenarios—such as imagining yourself on a beach or walking through a beautiful forest—can help deepen the trance and

encourage relaxation. The more detailed the imagery, the more effective it becomes.

4. **Affirmations and Suggestions**: Once in a relaxed state, the individual can introduce positive affirmations or suggestions that align with their desired outcome. These might include statements such as "I am confident and calm" or "I am in control of my actions." By repeating these affirmations, they become embedded in the subconscious mind.

5. **Counting Down**: Another method for entering self-hypnosis is through counting. This technique involves slowly counting down from 10 to 1 (or any other number), with each number helping the individual to relax more deeply. The act of counting, paired with the focus on relaxation, guides the person into a hypnotic state.

Applications of Self-Hypnosis

Self-hypnosis is a versatile tool that can be applied to many different areas of life. It is used for both therapeutic purposes and personal development. Some common applications include:

1. **Stress Management**: One of the most widely used benefits of self-hypnosis is its ability to reduce stress and promote relaxation. By using self-hypnosis techniques, individuals can calm their minds, relax their bodies, and reduce the physiological effects of stress. This can lead to a greater sense of calm, improved emotional well-being, and a reduction in anxiety.

2. **Overcoming Unwanted Habits**: Whether it's smoking, overeating, or nail biting, self-hypnosis can help break unwanted habits. The process allows individuals to reframe their thought patterns and create new, healthier behaviors. Through repeated sessions, the subconscious mind adopts new ways of thinking and reacting, replacing old, detrimental habits with new ones.

3. **Improved Sleep**: Self-hypnosis is often used to address issues like insomnia or disrupted sleep. By relaxing the mind and body before bedtime, self-hypnosis helps create a peaceful mental environment conducive to sleep. Visualizations, calming suggestions, and deep breathing can all contribute to better sleep quality.

4. **Pain Management**: Self-hypnosis can also be effective for managing chronic pain or discomfort. By focusing on relaxation and using mental techniques to distance oneself from the sensation of pain, individuals can reduce the intensity of pain and improve their tolerance. It's often used alongside other pain management strategies in both chronic conditions and acute pain episodes.

5. **Enhancing Performance**: Athletes and performers often use self-hypnosis to improve their focus and performance. Through visualization and positive suggestions, individuals can boost their self-confidence, sharpen their concentration, and overcome mental barriers that may hinder their success.

6. **Overcoming Fears and Phobias**: Self-hypnosis is a useful tool for addressing irrational fears or phobias. By accessing the subconscious, individuals can explore the root causes of their fears and reframe their emotional responses. This helps reduce the intensity of the fear and allows the person to face situations they may have once avoided.

Benefits of Self-Hypnosis

Self-hypnosis is a simple, natural, and non-invasive tool for personal growth and healing. Some of the primary benefits include:

- **Self-Empowerment**: Self-hypnosis gives individuals the ability to make lasting changes in their lives without relying on outside help. By learning to control the mind and direct it toward positive outcomes, people gain a sense of control and empowerment over their own mental and emotional states.
- **Cost-Effective**: Unlike therapy or medication, self-hypnosis is a cost-free practice once the necessary skills are learned. With regular practice, individuals can become more self-sufficient in managing issues like stress, anxiety, or unwanted behaviors.
- **Improved Focus and Clarity**: By training the mind to focus, self-hypnosis can help individuals gain clarity in decision-making, improve concentration, and increase productivity in daily tasks.
- **Relaxation and Well-Being**: The act of practicing self-hypnosis, even for a short time each day, can help individuals cultivate a deeper sense of peace and relaxation, reducing the negative effects of stress on both the body and mind.

Is Self-Hypnosis for Everyone?

Self-hypnosis can be effective for most people, but it does require some practice and patience. The ability to enter a deep hypnotic state varies from person to person, and some may find it difficult to achieve the necessary level of focus or relaxation without guidance. For those who struggle with self-hypnosis, working with a trained hypnotherapist can be beneficial. Over time, with consistent effort and guidance, many individuals can master the techniques and use self-hypnosis effectively on their own.

Conclusion

Self-hypnosis is a valuable tool for anyone looking to improve their mental well-being, change behaviors, or enhance their overall quality of life. By learning to enter a relaxed, focused state and harness the power of the subconscious mind, individuals can achieve lasting positive changes. Whether it's managing stress, overcoming fears, breaking habits, or improving performance, self-hypnosis provides a simple, effective way to take control of one's thoughts and behaviors. With practice and dedication, anyone can learn how to use self-hypnosis to create a healthier, more empowered life.

Techniques for Self-Hypnosis

Self-hypnosis is a valuable skill that anyone can learn, helping individuals to access the subconscious mind to make positive changes. The process involves inducing a deeply relaxed, focused state where the subconscious becomes more receptive to suggestions and affirmations. While self-hypnosis can be a straightforward practice, it requires some skill and consistency to master. There are several techniques that can guide you into a hypnotic state and ensure that you're able to utilize it effectively for personal growth, relaxation, and behavior modification.

Progressive Relaxation

One of the most widely used methods for inducing self-hypnosis is progressive relaxation. This technique involves progressively relaxing each muscle group in the body to release physical tension and enter a calm, trance-like state.

To practice this, begin by sitting or lying down in a comfortable position. Focus on your feet, and as you inhale, tense the muscles slightly for a few seconds, then exhale and allow them to relax completely. Gradually work your way up through your body, from the feet to the head, relaxing each muscle group in turn. As you do this, keep your focus on the physical sensations of relaxation and release, letting your body sink deeper into calmness with each breath.

Deep Breathing

Deep breathing is a simple yet effective technique that is often used to induce relaxation before entering hypnosis. The goal is to slow down your breathing and focus your attention solely on the rhythm of your inhales and exhales.

To begin, sit in a comfortable position and take a few deep breaths, slowly inhaling through the nose for a count of four, holding the breath for a moment, and then exhaling through the mouth for a count of four. Continue this process, gradually lengthening the time of each breath, until you begin to feel calm and focused. Deep breathing helps to activate the parasympathetic nervous system, promoting relaxation and preparing the mind for hypnosis.

Visualization

Visualization, or mental imagery, is another powerful tool for self-hypnosis. This technique involves imagining a calming scene or an ideal outcome that aligns with your goals. By immersing yourself in vivid mental images, you can guide your mind into a more focused, suggestible state.

To use visualization, first find a quiet space and relax your body. Close your eyes and imagine a peaceful scene, such as a beach, a forest, or a mountaintop. Focus on the details—feel the warmth of the sun, hear the sound of the waves, or notice the scent of pine trees. Engaging all the senses in your visualization helps create a more immersive experience, which deepens the hypnotic state. As you focus on the scene, you can also introduce positive suggestions related to your goals, reinforcing the changes you want to make.

4. Counting Down

Counting down is a simple technique that can help focus the mind and deepen the hypnotic state. This method works by guiding the individual into relaxation and increasing their mental suggestibility through the act of counting.

Start by closing your eyes and taking a few deep breaths to relax. Begin counting backward slowly from 10 to 1, allowing your body and mind to relax more with each number. As you count, imagine yourself becoming more deeply relaxed, sinking into a state of calm and focus. With each number, allow yourself to feel heavier and more relaxed, as though the number itself is a step toward a deeper state of hypnosis.

5. Eye Fixation

Eye fixation is another method used to enter self-hypnosis. This technique involves focusing your attention on a specific object or point, allowing your eyes to become tired and relaxed. The idea is that prolonged focus on a single point can help calm the mind and induce a trance-like state.

To use eye fixation, choose an object or spot in the room, such as a candle flame, a picture, or a spot on the wall. Focus all your attention on this point and try not to blink or move your eyes. As you concentrate, your eyes will naturally begin to tire, and this will help you relax further. The more deeply you focus, the easier it will be to enter a hypnotic trance. Once you feel your mind becoming calm and your body relaxing, you can introduce suggestions or affirmations.

6. Self-Suggestion and Affirmations

Once in a relaxed state, the next step is to introduce positive self-suggestions or affirmations. This is where the power of the subconscious mind comes into play. During hypnosis, the mind is more open to new ideas, and repetitive suggestions can help change limiting beliefs or unwanted behaviors.

To begin, choose a simple, positive statement that reflects the change you wish to make. For example, if you're aiming to overcome anxiety, you might use the affirmation, "I am calm and in control." If you're focused on weight loss, you might repeat, "I make healthy choices and feel strong." As you repeat the suggestion, allow yourself to fully believe in it and visualize the desired outcome. Repeating these affirmations during hypnosis helps reinforce new patterns of thought and behavior.

7. Anchoring

Anchoring is a technique that links a physical gesture or action to a specific mental state. This process can be used during self-hypnosis to trigger relaxation or positive emotions whenever needed.

To use anchoring, first enter a relaxed state using one of the techniques mentioned above. Once you are deeply relaxed, choose a physical gesture—such as pressing your thumb and forefinger together, tapping your knuckles, or touching a specific spot on your body. As you do this, introduce a positive suggestion, such as, "I feel completely calm and relaxed." By repeating this process multiple times, the physical gesture becomes an "anchor" that can trigger the same relaxed state whenever used in the future.

8. Positive Visualization of Goals

Visualization can also be used not just for relaxation, but also for achieving specific goals. This technique involves imagining the successful achievement of a goal as if it's already happening.

For example, if your goal is to speak confidently in public, you would close your eyes, relax, and visualize yourself standing in front of an audience, speaking confidently and clearly. As you visualize the event, focus on how you feel—calm, confident, and in control. The more vivid and real you make the scenario, the more effective this visualization becomes in helping to create the desired change.

Conclusion

These self-hypnosis techniques provide various ways to guide the mind into a deeply relaxed, focused state, making it receptive to positive change. Whether you're using self-hypnosis for stress management, breaking habits, enhancing performance, or achieving personal goals, these methods can help you access the power of your subconscious mind. While practice is key, anyone can learn to use these techniques and experience the benefits of self-hypnosis for mental, emotional, and physical well-being.

Potential Risks and Benefits

Hypnosis is often viewed as a tool for personal development, therapeutic healing, and relaxation, but like any technique, it comes with both potential benefits and risks. When used correctly, hypnosis can offer transformative results, but it is important to understand how it works and when it might be inappropriate or potentially harmful.

Benefits of Hypnosis

1. **Stress Reduction and Relaxation**
   Hypnosis is widely regarded for its ability to induce deep relaxation and reduce stress. By entering a state of focused concentration, the individual can lower levels of the stress hormone cortisol and activate the body's parasympathetic nervous system. This can lead to a sense of calm, improved sleep quality, and a reduction in anxiety. For those with chronic stress, regular use of hypnosis can help prevent the physical and mental health effects of prolonged stress.
2. **Pain Management**
   Hypnosis has been used successfully as part of pain management protocols, particularly for chronic pain conditions like arthritis, fibromyalgia, and migraines. It works by shifting the focus away from the pain and using suggestion to alter the perception of discomfort. Research suggests that hypnosis can reduce pain intensity and improve tolerance to pain, making it a non-invasive option for pain relief.
3. **Behavioral Change**
   One of the most commonly cited benefits of hypnosis is its ability to help people change unwanted behaviors. This includes smoking cessation, weight loss, reducing nail-biting, and overcoming phobias. Hypnosis allows individuals to access the subconscious mind, where habits are formed, and introduce new, positive suggestions that replace old patterns. The relaxed state during hypnosis makes it easier to accept these suggestions, leading to lasting behavioral change.
4. **Improved Sleep**
   Hypnosis can be an effective tool for overcoming insomnia and other sleep disorders. By calming the mind and promoting a state of relaxation, hypnosis makes it easier to fall asleep and stay asleep. Techniques such as deep breathing, progressive relaxation, and visualization are often used to quiet racing thoughts and prepare the body for restful sleep.
5. **Mental Clarity and Focus**
   Hypnosis can help improve concentration and mental clarity by reducing

distractions and sharpening focus. This can be particularly beneficial for individuals who struggle with attention disorders or those looking to enhance their cognitive performance. Athletes and students, for example, can use hypnosis to visualize success, boost their motivation, and stay mentally focused on their goals.

6. **Emotional Healing**
   For some, hypnosis provides a pathway to emotional healing. It can help individuals process past trauma, confront fears, and explore unresolved emotions in a safe, controlled environment. By allowing access to deeper layers of the subconscious, hypnosis can help people address the root causes of anxiety, depression, and other emotional struggles.

1. **False Memories**
   One of the risks associated with hypnosis is the potential for false memories, also known as confabulation. When individuals are in a deeply suggestible state, they may begin to "remember" events that didn't actually occur, or reconstruct details of past experiences in a way that is inaccurate. This is particularly problematic in therapeutic settings, where individuals might believe they have recovered repressed memories, even though these memories may be fabricated. It's important for anyone undergoing hypnotherapy to work with a qualified, ethical practitioner who understands the potential for memory distortion.

2. **Dependency on the Hypnotherapist**
   While hypnosis can be an empowering tool, there's a potential for individuals to become overly reliant on a hypnotherapist or the process itself. If hypnosis is used as a crutch for managing everyday life or addressing personal issues, individuals may not develop the coping skills or self-reliance needed for long-term well-being. In some cases, people might feel like they cannot solve problems or make changes without the aid of hypnosis.

3. **Negative Emotional Reactions**
   Some people may experience negative emotional reactions during hypnosis, especially if they are revisiting trauma or confronting deeply suppressed emotions. Although this can sometimes lead to breakthroughs, it can also trigger overwhelming emotions such as fear, guilt, or sadness. This is why it's essential for hypnosis to be conducted in a safe environment, preferably under the guidance of a trained and experienced therapist.

4. **Not Suitable for Everyone**
   Hypnosis may not be effective or suitable for everyone. People with certain mental health disorders, such as schizophrenia or severe personality disorders, may not respond well to hypnosis. Individuals with certain types of cognitive impairments or those who are highly resistant to suggestion may also find hypnosis less effective. Additionally, some people may simply have difficulty entering a deep enough state of relaxation to experience the benefits of hypnosis.

5. **Untrained Practitioners**
    A major risk of hypnosis is the potential for unethical or unqualified practitioners.
    While many licensed therapists and clinicians are trained in hypnosis, there is also
    a growing number of untrained individuals offering hypnotherapy services.
    Without proper training, a practitioner may inadvertently cause harm, such as
    implanting false suggestions or creating confusion. It's crucial to verify that the
    practitioner is licensed and has appropriate credentials before undergoing
    hypnosis.

Conclusion

Hypnosis can offer significant benefits, from stress reduction and pain management to
behavioral changes and emotional healing. When practiced properly, it serves as a
powerful tool for improving well-being and addressing a wide range of mental and
physical health concerns. However, like any therapeutic modality, it's important to be
aware of the potential risks, including the possibility of false memories, dependency, and
negative emotional reactions. To mitigate these risks, hypnosis should be performed by
trained professionals who create a safe, supportive environment. By understanding both
the advantages and potential drawbacks, individuals can use hypnosis in a way that
enhances their lives and promotes lasting positive change.

Hypnosis in Therapy

Hypnosis has been recognized as a powerful therapeutic tool, utilized by trained professionals to treat a variety of psychological and physical issues. In a therapeutic setting, hypnosis involves guiding a person into a state of deep relaxation and focused concentration, often referred to as a trance, where they are more receptive to suggestions. This heightened suggestibility allows the therapist to work directly with the subconscious mind, helping the individual address problems that might be difficult to access through traditional conscious thought processes.

Applications of Hypnosis in Therapy

1. **Pain Management**
   Hypnosis is frequently used in pain management, especially for chronic pain conditions such as fibromyalgia, arthritis, and migraines. In a hypnotic state, individuals can alter their perception of pain, shifting focus away from the discomfort and, in some cases, numbing or reducing its intensity. This method is particularly beneficial for people who want to avoid or reduce their reliance on pain medications. It has also been used in procedures such as dental work and childbirth to reduce pain and anxiety, known as "hypnoanalgesia."
2. **Treatment of Anxiety and Stress**
   Hypnosis has been shown to be effective in managing anxiety and stress. By inducing a deep state of relaxation, hypnosis helps reduce the levels of stress hormones like cortisol. Through relaxation and focused imagery, individuals can learn to control the physical symptoms of anxiety, such as rapid heartbeat and shallow breathing. Furthermore, hypnosis can aid in addressing the root causes of stress, such as unresolved emotional issues or past traumas, allowing patients to confront and process these concerns in a safe and controlled manner.
3. **Overcoming Phobias**
   One of the more impressive uses of hypnosis is in the treatment of phobias. Phobias are often deeply embedded in the subconscious mind, making them resistant to traditional therapies. Hypnosis can help individuals confront and reframe their irrational fears by accessing the subconscious mind and reprogramming the emotional response. Through techniques such as systematic desensitization or visualization, the therapist can help a patient gradually overcome the triggers of their phobia, leading to lasting relief.
4. **Behavioral Modifications**
   Hypnosis is commonly used to help individuals modify undesirable behaviors,

including smoking, overeating, and nail-biting. During a hypnotherapy session, th
therapist works with the subconscious to reinforce positive behaviors and change
old, detrimental patterns. For example, a person attempting to quit smoking might
be given suggestions to replace the urge to smoke with a healthier activity, such a
drinking water or going for a walk. With consistent practice, these suggestions car
become integrated into the individual's daily life, making it easier to break free
from harmful habits.

5. **Sleep Disorders**

   Hypnosis is often used as a tool to address insomnia and other sleep disorders. In
   therapeutic settings, hypnosis helps calm an overactive mind, promoting relaxatio
   and the natural sleep cycle. Through guided visualization and deep relaxation
   techniques, the therapist helps the patient develop better sleep habits and
   reprogram the subconscious mind to associate bedtime with relaxation rather than
   anxiety or restlessness. As a result, many people who suffer from insomnia or
   other sleep disturbances find significant relief through hypnotherapy.

6. **Trauma and PTSD**

   For those dealing with trauma or post-traumatic stress disorder (PTSD), hypnosis
   offers a way to access and process painful memories and emotions. In a hypnotic
   state, individuals can safely revisit traumatic events without the emotional
   overwhelm that typically occurs in conscious recollection. With the guidance of a
   trained therapist, they can work through past trauma, reframe negative
   associations, and create healthier emotional responses. Hypnosis has been
   successfully used as part of a broader therapeutic approach for PTSD, offering
   long-term relief and healing.

7. **Improving Self-Esteem and Confidence**

   Hypnotherapy is also used to address issues related to self-esteem and confidence.
   Many individuals carry negative self-beliefs that stem from past experiences,
   societal pressures, or childhood conditioning. Hypnosis can help reprogram these
   limiting beliefs by introducing positive affirmations and visualizations of success
   and self-worth. For example, a person with low self-esteem may be guided to
   imagine themselves as confident, successful, and worthy of success, which can
   lead to significant improvements in self-perception and behavior.

How Hypnotherapy Works

In a typical hypnotherapy session, the therapist first works with the client to establish
trust and ensure they are comfortable. This is essential, as a relaxed and open state of
mind is necessary for hypnosis to be effective. The therapist then guides the client into a
deeply relaxed state, often through progressive relaxation or focused breathing exercises.
Once the individual is in a trance, the therapist uses suggestions, imagery, or metaphors
to address the issue at hand.

For example, when treating stress, the therapist might suggest that the client imagine a peaceful and calming place, focusing on each sensory detail—sight, sound, and touch. These mental exercises can help the client let go of tension and redirect their thoughts in a positive direction. During this process, the therapist may also offer affirmations and suggestions designed to create positive change, such as helping the client to see themselves as confident or in control.

The process typically ends with the therapist gently guiding the client back to full awareness, reinforcing the positive changes made during the session. Many clients experience a feeling of calm and increased clarity after a session, and repeated sessions may be required to address deeper issues or achieve lasting results.

Limitations of Hypnosis in Therapy

While hypnosis has many therapeutic benefits, it is not a universal cure-all. The success of hypnotherapy depends on the individual's receptivity to the process, their willingness to embrace the therapy, and the skill of the practitioner. Not everyone is equally susceptible to hypnosis, and some individuals may find it difficult to enter the trance-like state required for therapeutic results. Additionally, hypnosis should not be seen as a substitute for traditional medical or psychological treatment in severe cases, such as acute mental illness or major physical health conditions. It is most effective when used as part of a holistic treatment plan.

Conclusion

Hypnosis is an effective therapeutic tool for a wide range of issues, from anxiety and pain management to behavioral changes and trauma recovery. By accessing the subconscious mind, hypnotherapy enables individuals to make lasting changes that might otherwise be difficult to achieve through conscious thought alone. When practiced by trained professionals, hypnosis can be a powerful and transformative experience, helping individuals lead healthier, more balanced lives. However, as with any therapeutic approach, it is important to approach hypnosis with a clear understanding of its limitations and to seek the guidance of qualified practitioners for optimal results.

The Role of Hypnosis in Psychotherapy

Hypnosis plays a unique and valuable role in psychotherapy, offering an alternative pathway to healing for individuals dealing with a variety of psychological issues. Unlike traditional talk therapy, which focuses on conscious thought and problem-solving, hypnosis allows therapists to access the subconscious mind—where many emotional and psychological issues are stored. This deeper level of access can facilitate profound therapeutic change, helping individuals overcome long-standing challenges such as trauma, anxiety, phobias, and negative thought patterns.

How Hypnosis Enhances Psychotherapy

1. **Accessing the Subconscious Mind**
   The core benefit of hypnosis in psychotherapy is its ability to bypass the critical conscious mind and directly access the subconscious. Many deeply rooted emotional problems—such as unresolved trauma, anxiety, or harmful beliefs—reside in the subconscious, making them difficult to address through regular conversation. In a hypnotic state, individuals are more open to exploring these hidden aspects of their psyche, allowing them to uncover the root causes of their difficulties. This process enables a deeper understanding of the issues at hand and allows for more targeted interventions.

2. **Reducing Resistance**
   In traditional therapy, clients may be resistant to confronting painful emotions or memories. This resistance is often due to the fear of reliving past trauma or the discomfort of facing difficult feelings. Hypnosis, however, helps lower this resistance by inducing a state of relaxation and focused attention, where the client feels more comfortable and in control. This state makes it easier for the therapist and client to explore sensitive topics without triggering the intense emotional reactions that might occur in a fully conscious state.

3. **Reframing Negative Thought Patterns**
   Hypnosis is particularly effective for individuals who struggle with negative thought patterns or self-destructive behaviors. In a relaxed, suggestible state, therapists can introduce new perspectives and positive affirmations that challenge the client's existing beliefs. For example, a person with low self-esteem may be encouraged to visualize themselves as confident and capable, or someone with chronic anxiety may be taught to reframe anxious thoughts as manageable and

under control. Over time, these suggestions can reshape the client's perceptions, leading to lasting changes in behavior and emotional well-being.

4. **Processing Trauma**
   One of the most powerful applications of hypnosis in psychotherapy is in the treatment of trauma. Traumatic memories, particularly those from childhood or significant life events, are often stored in the subconscious in a fragmented or distorted way. Hypnosis allows clients to access these memories safely and with greater emotional control, which can be crucial for individuals with post-traumatic stress disorder (PTSD). By revisiting and reframing these experiences in a controlled and supportive environment, clients can begin to process the trauma, release the emotional charge associated with it, and ultimately heal.

5. **Overcoming Phobias and Anxiety**
   Hypnosis is an effective tool for treating various types of anxiety and phobias. These issues are often driven by irrational fears or deeply embedded thought patterns, which the subconscious mind reinforces over time. In hypnosis, therapists can help clients confront their fears in a gradual, controlled manner. For example, a person with a fear of flying might be guided to imagine taking a flight in a relaxed state, gradually reducing their anxiety as they become desensitized to the idea of flying. By introducing positive suggestions and reframing the emotional response to the phobia, hypnosis can significantly reduce or eliminate irrational fears.

6. **Enhancing Emotional Regulation**
   Hypnosis can also help individuals regulate their emotions by teaching them to access a calm, centered state during times of stress or emotional upheaval. People who struggle with impulsive behaviors, anger issues, or emotional dysregulation can benefit from learning how to induce a relaxed, focused state through hypnosis. This mental training helps individuals gain control over their emotional responses, creating greater emotional stability and resilience. By teaching clients to manage their reactions and stress more effectively, hypnosis enhances their overall ability to cope with life's challenges.

7. **Improving Self-Image and Confidence**
   Many individuals with issues such as low self-esteem, body image concerns, or performance anxiety benefit from the use of hypnosis in psychotherapy. Hypnotic techniques can help individuals access and reinforce their inner strengths, allowing them to envision themselves as competent, confident, and capable of achieving their goals. By reframing negative self-talk and building a stronger, more positive self-image, clients can experience a significant boost in confidence and self-worth. In some cases, hypnosis can even help individuals overcome mental blocks related to performance, such as public speaking anxiety or writer's block.

Integrating Hypnosis with Traditional Psychotherapy

While hypnosis can be an incredibly powerful therapeutic tool, it is most effective when integrated into a broader psychotherapy approach. Hypnosis is not meant to replace traditional psychotherapy; rather, it enhances the work being done in a conventional therapeutic setting. Many therapists combine hypnosis with other therapeutic modalities, such as cognitive-behavioral therapy (CBT), psychodynamic therapy, or trauma-focused therapy, to create a comprehensive treatment plan tailored to the individual's needs.

The use of hypnosis in psychotherapy requires specialized training and expertise, as it involves guiding the client into a deep state of relaxation and then making suggestions that can lead to lasting change. It is essential that the therapist be well-versed in both the theory and practical application of hypnosis, ensuring that the process is ethical, safe, and effective.

The Potential Limitations of Hypnosis in Psychotherapy

Despite its many benefits, hypnosis is not a one-size-fits-all solution. The effectiveness of hypnosis depends largely on the client's ability to enter a hypnotic state, which varies from person to person. Some individuals are more easily hypnotized than others, and those who are highly resistant to suggestion may not experience the same level of benefit. Additionally, hypnosis may not be suitable for individuals with certain psychological conditions, such as severe dissociative disorders or certain types of personality disorders, which may make it more difficult to access the subconscious mind in a safe and controlled manner.

Moreover, the success of hypnosis in psychotherapy often requires a strong therapeutic alliance between the client and therapist. A trusting, collaborative relationship is essential for hypnosis to be effective, as clients need to feel comfortable and safe while exploring deep-seated emotions or past trauma.

Conclusion

Hypnosis in psychotherapy offers a unique and powerful way to address a variety of psychological issues. By accessing the subconscious mind, hypnosis allows therapists to help clients process trauma, change negative thought patterns, overcome phobias, and improve emotional regulation. When integrated into a comprehensive therapeutic plan, hypnosis can enhance the effectiveness of traditional psychotherapy, leading to lasting changes and improved mental health. However, as with any therapeutic approach, it is important for individuals to work with qualified professionals who understand the nuances and limitations of hypnosis, ensuring that it is used in a safe and ethical manner.

Hypnotherapy and Cognitive Therapy

Hypnotherapy and cognitive therapy are two distinct but complementary therapeutic approaches used to treat a wide range of psychological conditions. While each method has its own unique techniques, combining elements of both can lead to more effective outcomes for clients. By utilizing hypnosis to access the subconscious mind and cognitive therapy to address conscious thoughts and behaviors, therapists can create a holistic treatment plan that tackles both the underlying emotional issues and the cognitive patterns contributing to the problem.

Hypnotherapy: Accessing the Subconscious Mind

Hypnotherapy involves guiding a person into a deep state of focused attention, often referred to as a trance. In this state, the conscious mind becomes more relaxed, while the subconscious mind is more open to suggestions. This allows the therapist to work directly with the subconscious, addressing issues that may be too deeply ingrained or difficult to reach through normal conscious thought processes. Hypnotherapy is particularly effective in treating conditions such as anxiety, phobias, trauma, and chronic pain, as it can help individuals access and resolve underlying emotional or psychological causes that may be buried in the subconscious.

Through the use of specific techniques, such as guided imagery, positive suggestions, and visualizations, hypnotherapy aims to shift the subconscious patterns and behaviors that are often at the root of emotional distress. For example, a person struggling with smoking addiction might be guided to envision themselves as a non-smoker in a variety of situations, while receiving positive suggestions to reinforce their new identity. By creating these new associations and reframing old beliefs, hypnotherapy can promote lasting behavioral change.

Cognitive Therapy: Changing Thoughts and Behaviors

Cognitive therapy, or cognitive-behavioral therapy (CBT), is a structured, goal-oriented approach that focuses on identifying and changing negative thought patterns and behaviors. The underlying premise of CBT is that our thoughts, emotions, and behaviors are interconnected, and that by changing the way we think, we can alter our emotional responses and behaviors. This approach is often used to treat conditions such as depression, anxiety, and obsessive-compulsive disorder (OCD), as it helps individuals recognize and challenge distorted or unhelpful thought patterns that contribute to their mental health struggles.

Cognitive therapy works by teaching clients to identify automatic negative thoughts (ANTs) and replace them with more balanced, realistic thinking. For example, a person with social anxiety might have the automatic thought, "I will embarrass myself if I speak in public." CBT helps individuals reframe this thought, perhaps by considering evidence that contradicts it, such as past successful experiences or the reality that most people are understanding and forgiving in social situations. Over time, clients learn to adopt healthier cognitive habits that reduce emotional distress and lead to positive behavioral changes.

Integrating Hypnotherapy and Cognitive Therapy

When combined, hypnotherapy and cognitive therapy offer a powerful approach to treatment, leveraging the strengths of both methods. Hypnotherapy can provide immediate access to the subconscious, helping to uncover and address deeply rooted emotional issues, while cognitive therapy offers a structured framework for changing negative thought patterns and behaviors in the conscious mind. This dual approach allow for a more comprehensive treatment plan that addresses both the underlying causes of distress and the day-to-day thought patterns that perpetuate it.

For instance, a client struggling with chronic anxiety may benefit from both approaches. Hypnotherapy could be used to help the client access and process past trauma or unresolved emotional conflicts contributing to their anxiety. Meanwhile, cognitive therapy could help the client recognize and challenge the distorted thoughts that fuel their anxious feelings, such as catastrophizing or overgeneralizing. Together, these methods work synergistically to provide relief from both the emotional and cognitive aspects of anxiety.

One key benefit of combining hypnotherapy with cognitive therapy is that hypnotherapy can enhance the effectiveness of cognitive techniques. In the relaxed, focused state of hypnosis, clients may be more open to the suggestions and insights provided through cognitive therapy, leading to deeper and more lasting changes. For example, a client in hypnosis might be guided to visualize themselves confidently handling a stressful situation, which reinforces the cognitive shifts they are learning through therapy.

Addressing Negative Behaviors and Thought Patterns

In cases of behavioral issues such as smoking, overeating, or chronic procrastination, integrating both therapies can lead to lasting change. Hypnotherapy can work to reprogram the subconscious mind, helping individuals to associate healthier behaviors with positive emotions. Cognitive therapy, on the other hand, can teach clients practical strategies for maintaining these changes, such as setting goals, managing triggers, and challenging any negative thoughts or beliefs that might arise during the process.

For example, someone who is trying to lose weight may benefit from hypnotherapy to strengthen their resolve and address subconscious beliefs that contribute to unhealthy eating habits. Cognitive therapy can then provide the tools to help them recognize and replace the thought patterns that lead to overeating, such as emotional eating or stress-related cravings. By working on both the conscious and subconscious levels, clients can develop a more sustainable approach to behavioral change.

The Synergistic Benefits of Both Approaches

The integration of hypnotherapy and cognitive therapy can offer several advantages over using either method alone. By addressing both the conscious and subconscious aspects of the mind, clients are able to make more comprehensive and lasting changes. Hypnotherapy provides the deep, transformative access to the subconscious that is necessary for addressing deeply rooted issues, while cognitive therapy offers the structured, practical tools needed to maintain and reinforce those changes in everyday life.

In addition, the combined approach can accelerate the healing process. For example, while cognitive therapy helps a client recognize and reframe negative thoughts, hypnotherapy can reinforce those changes by embedding new, positive beliefs into the subconscious mind. This can lead to quicker and more lasting improvements in mental health and well-being, as both conscious and subconscious minds work in harmony.

Conclusion

The integration of hypnotherapy and cognitive therapy offers a dynamic and effective treatment approach for a wide range of psychological issues. Hypnotherapy allows access to the subconscious mind, helping to uncover and resolve deep-seated emotional issues, while cognitive therapy addresses the conscious thought patterns and behaviors that contribute to psychological distress. When used together, these approaches can complement each other, leading to lasting and transformative change. For individuals seeking a comprehensive approach to mental health, the combination of hypnotherapy and cognitive therapy provides a powerful toolkit for healing and personal growth.

Examining The Effectiveness of Hypnotherapy

Hypnotherapy has gained significant attention in recent years as an effective treatment for various psychological and physical conditions. By utilizing the power of the subconscious mind, hypnotherapy aims to address deep-rooted issues that may not be easily accessed through traditional therapeutic approaches. The effectiveness of hypnotherapy depends on numerous factors, including the skill of the therapist, the client's suggestibility, and the nature of the issue being treated. Research has shown promising results in several areas, demonstrating its potential as a valuable therapeutic tool.

Effectiveness in Treating Anxiety and Stress

One of the most well-established uses of hypnotherapy is in the treatment of anxiety and stress. The process of hypnosis helps induce a deeply relaxed state in which the body's stress response is minimized, while the mind becomes more open to positive suggestions. Numerous studies have indicated that hypnotherapy can significantly reduce symptoms of anxiety, especially in individuals with generalized anxiety disorder (GAD), social anxiety, or phobias. By addressing the subconscious causes of anxiety—such as past trauma or negative beliefs—hypnotherapy can help reframe these thoughts, leading to more positive emotional states and better coping mechanisms.

Additionally, hypnotherapy has shown effectiveness in managing the physical symptoms of stress, such as elevated blood pressure, muscle tension, and sleep disturbances. Clients often report feeling more relaxed, focused, and better able to manage their stress after undergoing hypnotherapy sessions.

Hypnotherapy for Pain Management

Hypnotherapy has long been recognized as a powerful tool for pain management. It is particularly effective for chronic pain conditions, such as fibromyalgia, arthritis, and headaches, as well as in managing pain during medical procedures like surgery or childbirth. Studies have demonstrated that individuals undergoing hypnotherapy report a significant reduction in pain intensity and emotional distress associated with chronic pain.

In a hypnotherapy session, the therapist may guide the client to visualize the pain as something that can be controlled or transformed. For example, the therapist might encourage the individual to imagine the pain as a color or shape that can be altered or removed. This process helps shift the focus away from the pain and allows the individual to feel more in control of their discomfort. Hypnosis also promotes the release of endorphins, the body's natural painkillers, which can further enhance pain relief.

Effectiveness for Behavioral Change

Hypnotherapy is widely used to help individuals change harmful behaviors such as smoking, overeating, and nail-biting. Research indicates that it can be highly effective for behaviors that are deeply ingrained, as it targets the subconscious mind where habits and patterns are formed. Hypnotherapy works by reprogramming the subconscious to adopt healthier behaviors and associations, such as a person visualizing themselves as a non-smoker or someone feeling satisfied with smaller portions of food.

A study published in the *Journal of Consulting and Clinical Psychology* found that hypnotherapy was more effective than other behavioral treatments for smoking cessation, with participants experiencing long-term success in quitting. Similarly, weight loss programs that incorporate hypnotherapy have been shown to yield better results than traditional dieting alone, as the therapy helps change the client's mindset around food and eating habits.

Treating Trauma and PTSD

Hypnotherapy is often used in the treatment of trauma and post-traumatic stress disorder (PTSD). It allows individuals to access repressed memories and emotions tied to past traumatic experiences in a controlled, safe environment. In a deeply relaxed state, the client can revisit the trauma without the overwhelming emotional reaction that might occur during conscious recollection. This makes it easier to process and reframe the memory, reducing its emotional charge.

Numerous studies have supported the use of hypnotherapy in trauma recovery, with patients showing significant improvement in their symptoms after undergoing hypnosis. This therapeutic approach can also reduce the frequency and severity of flashbacks and nightmares, which are common in PTSD.

Addressing Sleep Disorders

Hypnotherapy has shown effectiveness in treating sleep disorders such as insomnia. In fact, a study published in *Sleep* found that individuals who underwent hypnotherapy experienced improved sleep quality and were able to fall asleep more easily compared to those who received no treatment. Hypnosis promotes relaxation, which helps reduce the mental and physical tension that often interferes with sleep.

During a hypnotherapy session, the therapist may guide the client through progressive relaxation techniques, visualization, or suggest positive affirmations to create a sense of calm and safety, which can facilitate better sleep. This can be especially helpful for individuals whose sleep difficulties are linked to stress, anxiety, or negative thought patterns.

Potential Limitations and Considerations

While hypnotherapy has demonstrated effectiveness in many areas, it is not a universal solution for all conditions. The success of hypnotherapy largely depends on the individual's susceptibility to hypnosis. Some people are naturally more suggestible and respond more readily to hypnotherapy, while others may find it challenging to enter a trance-like state. This variability means that hypnotherapy may not be effective for everyone.

Additionally, hypnotherapy should not be considered a substitute for medical treatment in cases of severe mental health disorders, such as schizophrenia or bipolar disorder. It is most effective when used in conjunction with other therapeutic modalities, and under the guidance of a trained and certified hypnotherapist.

The Future of Hypnotherapy

The growing body of research supporting the effectiveness of hypnotherapy suggests that its role in healthcare and psychology will continue to expand. As scientific understanding of the brain and the subconscious deepens, new techniques and applications for hypnotherapy are likely to emerge. With increasing recognition of its potential to treat a wide range of conditions, more healthcare professionals may incorporate hypnotherapy into their treatment plans, providing patients with a powerful and non-invasive alternative to traditional therapies.

Conclusion

Hypnotherapy has proven to be a valuable therapeutic tool in the treatment of a variety of psychological and physical conditions. From managing anxiety and stress to reducing pain and addressing behavioral habits, hypnotherapy offers unique benefits by accessing the subconscious mind. While it may not be suitable for everyone, research consistently supports its effectiveness in numerous areas, making it a promising and complementary treatment for individuals seeking alternative or adjunctive therapies. As more studies emerge and techniques evolve, hypnotherapy's potential as a powerful tool for healing and personal growth will likely continue to grow.

Hypnotherapy Practice

Hypnotherapy practice is a specialized field that involves using hypnosis as a therapeutic tool to help individuals overcome a variety of psychological and physical challenges. The practice requires a deep understanding of both the hypnotic process and the underlying psychological conditions it aims to treat. Hypnotherapists work with clients to facilitate access to the subconscious mind, where deeply rooted patterns, beliefs, and memories can be addressed and transformed. While it may seem like a mysterious or mystical practice to some, hypnotherapy is grounded in science and is recognized by health professionals for its therapeutic potential.

The Hypnotherapy Process

The hypnotherapy process typically begins with an initial consultation, where the therapist assesses the client's needs, concerns, and goals. This is an important step, as it helps the therapist develop a tailored approach to treatment. During the consultation, the therapist will explain what hypnosis is, address any misconceptions, and discuss the specific techniques that may be used. This is also an opportunity for the client to ask questions and express any concerns about the process.

Once the client is ready to begin, the hypnotherapist will guide them into a relaxed, focused state known as a trance. This state is often described as a deep state of concentration, where the conscious mind is temporarily quieted, and the subconscious mind becomes more receptive to positive suggestions and therapeutic interventions. It's important to note that the client remains fully aware of their surroundings during hypnosis and cannot be made to do anything against their will. The hypnotherapist's role is to help the client achieve a state of relaxation where they can access the subconscious and work on their specific issues.

Techniques Used in Hypnotherapy

Several techniques are used in hypnotherapy, depending on the client's needs and the goals of treatment. Some of the most common methods include:

- **Progressive Relaxation:** This is often used to induce a trance-like state. The therapist guides the client through a series of steps that progressively relax different parts of the body, from the toes to the head. This helps to calm the mind

and create a sense of deep relaxation, which is necessary for effective
hypnotherapy.
- **Visualization:** During hypnosis, the therapist may guide the client to imagine
  certain scenarios, such as visualizing themselves overcoming a fear or achieving a
  goal. This can help to reframe negative thought patterns and create positive
  associations in the subconscious mind.
- **Positive Suggestion:** This involves providing the client with affirmations or
  suggestions that are designed to promote positive change. For example, someone
  trying to quit smoking might receive suggestions like, "You feel confident and in
  control when you are around others who smoke," or "You enjoy being healthy and
  free from nicotine."
- **Regression:** In some cases, hypnotherapists may use regression techniques to help
  clients access memories or experiences from the past. This can be particularly
  useful for addressing trauma, phobias, or other issues that are rooted in earlier life
  experiences. The therapist guides the client to revisit specific memories in a safe
  and controlled environment, helping them process and reframe the experience.
- **Ego Strengthening:** This technique helps to build confidence and self-esteem by
  guiding the client to visualize themselves handling situations with greater strength
  and resilience. The goal is to reinforce positive self-beliefs and empower the client
  to take charge of their thoughts and behaviors.

Applications of Hypnotherapy

Hypnotherapy can be used to treat a wide range of conditions, both psychological and
physical. Some common applications include:

- **Stress and Anxiety Reduction:** Hypnotherapy is particularly effective for
  individuals suffering from anxiety or stress. By inducing a deeply relaxed state,
  hypnotherapy helps to activate the body's natural relaxation response, reducing the
  physical and emotional symptoms of stress. It can also help individuals address the
  root causes of their anxiety, whether they are linked to past trauma, negative
  thought patterns, or ongoing life circumstances.
- **Pain Management:** Hypnotherapy has been widely used for pain relief,
  particularly for chronic pain conditions such as arthritis, fibromyalgia, and back
  pain. The practice helps clients reframe their perception of pain, teaching them
  techniques to reduce discomfort and increase tolerance. In medical settings,
  hypnotherapy has been used successfully during procedures like surgery or
  childbirth to reduce the need for medication and promote faster healing.
- **Behavioral Change:** Hypnotherapy is commonly used for behavior modification,
  such as smoking cessation, weight loss, or overcoming addictions. By working
  with the subconscious mind, hypnotherapy can help individuals break free from
  unhealthy habits and replace them with more positive, sustainable behaviors.

- **Trauma and PTSD:** Hypnotherapy is an effective tool for trauma recovery, as it allows individuals to process painful memories in a safe and controlled environment. This can be particularly helpful for those suffering from post-traumatic stress disorder (PTSD), as it helps them confront and reframe traumatic experiences without the overwhelming emotional reactions that might occur during traditional talk therapy.
- **Improving Sleep:** For individuals suffering from insomnia or other sleep disorders, hypnotherapy can promote better sleep by addressing the mental and emotional factors that interfere with rest. Hypnotherapy can help the client relax, manage stress, and change thought patterns that contribute to sleep disturbances.

Training and Certification for Hypnotherapists

Hypnotherapy is a specialized field that requires thorough training and certification. In order to practice legally and ethically, hypnotherapists must undergo comprehensive training programs, which can range from several months to years, depending on the depth of the course. These programs typically include both theoretical knowledge and hands-on practice, where students learn about the psychology of hypnosis, therapeutic techniques, and how to work with clients.

In many countries, hypnotherapists are required to be certified by a recognized professional organization, such as the American Society of Clinical Hypnosis (ASCH) or the British Society of Clinical Hypnosis (BSCH). Certification ensures that the hypnotherapist has received appropriate training and adheres to ethical guidelines, offering clients a safe and effective therapeutic experience.

Ethics and Professionalism in Hypnotherapy

As with any form of therapy, professionalism and ethics play a crucial role in hypnotherapy practice. Hypnotherapists must maintain strict boundaries, respect their clients' autonomy, and ensure that they do not use hypnosis for manipulative or unethical purposes. Informed consent is essential, and clients should always be made aware of the goals and methods of hypnotherapy before the process begins.

Hypnotherapists should also avoid making false claims or promises about the results of hypnotherapy. While many clients experience significant positive changes, the effectiveness of hypnosis can vary depending on the individual and their specific issues. Ethical hypnotherapists work collaboratively with clients to set realistic goals and monitor progress over time.

Conclusion

Hypnotherapy practice is a powerful therapeutic tool that can be used to address a wide range of psychological and physical conditions. By working with the subconscious mind, hypnotherapists can help individuals achieve deep relaxation, modify behavior, manage pain, and overcome emotional challenges. The practice requires skilled training and adherence to ethical guidelines to ensure that clients receive the highest standard of care. As awareness and understanding of hypnosis continue to grow, hypnotherapy is likely to remain an effective, non-invasive approach to improving mental and physical health.

Establishing a Hypnotherapy Practice

Starting a hypnotherapy practice is a rewarding endeavor that combines the art of helping people with the science of behavioral change. It requires careful planning, professional training, and a deep understanding of the ethical and practical considerations involved in running a therapy business. Whether you're transitioning from a career in psychology, counseling, or another health-related field, or you're starting fresh, establishing a hypnotherapy practice involves a clear roadmap to success.

1. Obtaining Proper Training and Certification

The first step in setting up a hypnotherapy practice is ensuring you have the proper training and certification. Hypnotherapy is a specialized field that requires thorough knowledge of human behavior, psychology, and hypnosis techniques. Training programs typically cover the history of hypnosis, the theories behind its effectiveness, induction and deepening methods, suggestion techniques, and how to work with clients to achieve therapeutic goals.

Certification from a reputable organization, such as the American Society of Clinical Hypnosis (ASCH), the National Guild of Hypnotists (NGH), or the British Society of Clinical Hypnosis (BSCH), is essential for establishing your credibility and ensuring you are recognized by clients and peers in the field. Many of these certifications require a combination of coursework, practical training, and supervised practice before you can become fully certified.

2. Defining Your Niche and Target Audience

One of the key elements of a successful hypnotherapy practice is understanding your target audience and defining your niche. Hypnotherapy can be applied to a wide range of issues, including stress and anxiety, pain management, smoking cessation, weight loss, trauma, and sleep disorders. Choosing a specific area of focus allows you to market your practice more effectively and position yourself as an expert in that area.

For instance, if you're particularly interested in helping individuals overcome anxiety or depression, you could specialize in those areas. Alternatively, if you're more drawn to pain management or behavioral modification, you might market yourself as a hypnotherapist for clients dealing with chronic pain or addiction. Having a clear niche helps attract clients who are seeking your specific expertise.

3. Creating a Business Plan

Like any business, establishing a hypnotherapy practice requires careful planning. A business plan serves as a blueprint for your practice and can help guide you through the initial stages, from setting goals to managing finances. Your business plan should include the following key components:

- **Mission and vision:** Define the purpose of your practice and the long-term goals you want to achieve.
- **Services offered:** Detail the types of hypnotherapy you'll provide (e.g., individual sessions, group sessions, workshops, etc.).
- **Market research:** Understand your local market and the demand for hypnotherapy services. Look at potential competitors, identify gaps in the market, and determine what sets your practice apart.
- **Pricing structure:** Determine how much you'll charge for your services, keeping in mind factors such as market rates, your level of expertise, and any special programs or packages you offer.
- **Financial projections:** Create a budget that includes startup costs (such as office space, marketing, and equipment), monthly expenses (rent, utilities, insurance, etc.), and expected income.

A well-thought-out business plan not only helps with the management of your practice but also increases the likelihood of securing funding if necessary.

4. Setting Up Your Practice Location

Choosing the right location is crucial when establishing a hypnotherapy practice. Many hypnotherapists choose to operate from a private office space where clients can feel comfortable and relaxed. It's important to select a location that is easily accessible, private, and professional, whether it's in a stand-alone office, a shared office space, or a wellness center.

If in-person consultations aren't feasible, consider offering remote hypnotherapy sessions through video conferencing platforms. Telehealth is becoming increasingly popular, and many clients find online sessions just as effective as in-person visits. Make sure your setup is secure, with high-quality video and audio equipment to provide the best experience for your clients.

5. Marketing and Building Clientele

Effective marketing is key to building a client base and growing your hypnotherapy practice. Start by creating a professional website that showcases your qualifications, services, and testimonials from clients (once you have built a client base). Your website should also include clear contact information and options for booking appointments.

ocial media platforms like Facebook, Instagram, and LinkedIn can be powerful tools for promoting your services and connecting with potential clients. Consider writing articles, log posts, or creating video content about hypnosis and how it can help people, as this an establish you as an expert in the field.

Networking with other healthcare professionals, such as therapists, counselors, doctors, r chiropractors, can also help expand your reach. By establishing professional elationships, you may receive referrals or collaborate on cases where hypnotherapy can e an adjunctive treatment.

Additionally, local advertising, such as flyers, business cards, or online listings, can help ou gain visibility within your community. You can also consider offering free workshops or group hypnotherapy sessions to introduce people to your services.

. Legal and Ethical Considerations

Before you begin seeing clients, it's important to ensure that your practice complies with ll legal and ethical requirements. This includes obtaining necessary licenses and nsurance, such as liability insurance, to protect yourself and your clients. Depending on our location, you may need to register your business, obtain a business license, and dhere to local health and safety regulations.

Ethics is also a critical aspect of hypnotherapy practice. Always ensure that you operate n a manner that respects client autonomy and confidentiality. You should maintain clear nd open communication with clients, discussing the goals of therapy, informed consent, nd the potential benefits and limitations of hypnotherapy. As a certified hypnotherapist, ou should adhere to the ethical guidelines set by your certification body and avoid naking unrealistic promises or guarantees about the outcomes of hypnotherapy.

. Continuing Education and Professional Development

As with any field, continuing education is vital to maintaining a successful hypnotherapy practice. Staying updated on the latest research, techniques, and best practices ensures ou remain effective in your work and provide the best possible service to your clients. Consider attending workshops, conferences, or pursuing advanced certifications to xpand your skills and knowledge.

Engaging in peer supervision or joining professional networks can provide valuable upport, feedback, and opportunities for growth. This can also help you stay motivated nd inspired as you continue to help clients improve their lives through hypnotherapy.

Conclusion

Establishing a hypnotherapy practice is a rewarding and impactful career choice for those
interested in the therapeutic use of hypnosis. By obtaining the right training and
certification, defining your niche, creating a business plan, and marketing your services,
you can build a successful practice that helps individuals overcome personal challenges
and achieve positive change. With the right dedication and expertise, hypnotherapy offer
a fulfilling way to make a meaningful difference in people's lives.

Ethics in Hypnotherapy

In the practice of hypnotherapy, ethics play a critical role in ensuring that clients receive safe, professional, and effective care. Hypnotherapists are trusted with the mental and emotional well-being of their clients, and as such, they are held to high ethical standards. These standards protect both the client and the therapist, fostering a relationship of trust, respect, and professionalism. Whether working with individuals to manage stress, overcome phobias, or break unhealthy habits, adhering to ethical guidelines is essential for delivering successful and responsible hypnotherapy.

Informed Consent

One of the foundational ethical principles in hypnotherapy is informed consent. Before beginning any therapeutic process, it is essential that the client fully understands the nature of hypnotherapy, the methods being used, and the goals of treatment. The hypnotherapist must explain the process in clear, understandable terms, outlining how hypnosis works, what the client can expect, and any potential risks or limitations of the treatment.

Informed consent also involves the client's right to ask questions and decide whether they want to proceed with therapy. A client must never be coerced or manipulated into undergoing hypnotherapy. This respect for autonomy ensures that the therapy is voluntary, and the client's consent is given freely without pressure.

Confidentiality and Privacy

Confidentiality is a cornerstone of all therapeutic practices, and hypnotherapy is no exception. Clients are often asked to share personal, vulnerable information during sessions. Hypnotherapists must keep all client information strictly confidential, including any details discussed during therapy or the content revealed while under hypnosis.

There are, however, certain legal exceptions to confidentiality. For example, if a client expresses intent to harm themselves or others, or if there is suspected abuse, the therapist may be legally required to disclose certain information to protect the client or others. These exceptions should be discussed with the client beforehand as part of the informed consent process.

Therapists should also ensure that records are securely stored, whether digitally or in paper form, to prevent unauthorized access to sensitive information. Maintaining privacy protects the integrity of the therapeutic relationship and reinforces trust.

Professional Boundaries

Maintaining professional boundaries is essential in any therapeutic relationship. Hypnotherapists must create a safe and respectful environment for clients to explore sensitive issues without fear of judgment or exploitation. These boundaries also extend to the physical environment, where therapists should be mindful of how they interact with clients, avoiding any actions that could be construed as inappropriate or invasive.

Physical touch is a sensitive area in hypnotherapy. While some therapies, like Reiki or certain body-focused techniques, may involve touch, hypnotherapists should approach this with caution and only with explicit consent. The client's comfort level must always be prioritized, and therapists should respect the client's personal space.

Avoiding Harm and Exploitation

Hypnotherapists must ensure that their practice does not cause harm to the client, either emotionally, mentally, or physically. Hypnosis should never be used to manipulate, deceive, or exploit clients for personal gain. For example, suggesting false memories or using hypnosis to pressure clients into making decisions that are not in their best interests is not only unethical, but also potentially harmful.

Ethical hypnotherapists should avoid offering guarantees about the outcomes of therapy, as results can vary based on the individual. It is important to make it clear that while hypnosis can be an effective tool, it is not a "quick fix" for deep-seated issues. Clients should be given realistic expectations of the therapy's potential.

Additionally, therapists should be vigilant about maintaining appropriate professional conduct at all times. This includes refraining from engaging in any form of relationship, whether personal or romantic, with clients during or after therapy. Such relationships could undermine the therapeutic process and violate ethical guidelines.

Competence and Professional Development

Hypnotherapists must practice within the scope of their competence, meaning they should only provide services for which they are properly trained and qualified. Continuing education is an essential part of ethical hypnotherapy practice, ensuring that therapists stay up-to-date with the latest techniques, research, and legal standards.

Hypnotherapists should also recognize their limitations. If a client's issue falls outside the therapist's area of expertise, it is ethically responsible to refer the client to another professional who may be better equipped to help. For instance, if a client presents with severe mental health conditions like schizophrenia or a history of trauma, the therapist may need to collaborate with a psychiatrist or psychologist before proceeding with hypnosis.

An ethical hypnotherapist must practice cultural competence, being aware of and sensitive to the client's background, beliefs, and values. This includes understanding how cultural factors may influence the client's perception of hypnosis and ensuring that any techniques or suggestions used are aligned with the client's worldview. Cultural sensitivity fosters a therapeutic environment in which clients feel respected and understood.

It's important for hypnotherapists to avoid making assumptions about a client's cultural or personal beliefs. Active listening and open communication can help build trust and ensure that therapy is tailored to the client's needs in a way that is respectful of their identity.

Ethical standards also apply to how hypnotherapists advertise their services. Therapists must ensure that their promotional materials accurately represent their qualifications and the services they offer. Misleading claims or exaggerated promises about the effectiveness of hypnotherapy are unethical and can damage the credibility of the profession.

For example, a hypnotherapist should not guarantee that they can cure a client's condition, such as chronic pain or a smoking habit, in a set number of sessions. Instead, they should focus on providing realistic expectations based on the individual's needs, treatment goals, and progress over time.

Hypnotherapists, like professionals in other fields, benefit from supervision and peer support. Ethical practice includes seeking advice or supervision when faced with challenging cases or when the therapist feels they need guidance. Engaging with a network of colleagues allows for professional development and helps maintain high standards of care.

Moreover, it's important for hypnotherapists to reflect on their own practices regularly, ensuring they are providing the best possible care for their clients. This may involve attending workshops, engaging in self-reflection, or consulting with more experienced practitioners.

Conclusion

The ethical practice of hypnotherapy is central to the well-being of clients and the integrity of the profession. By adhering to the principles of informed consent, confidentiality, professional boundaries, competence, and cultural sensitivity, hypnotherapists ensure that they are providing effective and responsible care. Upholding these ethical standards not only protects clients, but also fosters a therapeutic environment of trust and respect, ensuring that hypnotherapy remains a valuable and respected form of therapy.

Children and Hypnosis

Hypnosis has long been recognized for its therapeutic potential in treating a wide range of conditions, from anxiety and pain management to habit-breaking. While hypnosis is commonly used with adults, it can also be highly effective for children. However, applying hypnosis with children requires a unique approach that is tailored to their developmental stage, emotional needs, and cognitive abilities.

How Children Respond to Hypnosis

Children tend to be more responsive to hypnosis than adults for several reasons. One of the key factors is their naturally vivid imaginations and heightened suggestibility. Children's minds are often more open and flexible, which makes them more receptive to the suggestions and creative visualizations involved in hypnosis. They also have a greater capacity for "fantasy thinking," which allows them to experience vivid, immersive imagery when guided by a hypnotherapist.

Additionally, children are less likely to have ingrained mental resistance or skepticism about hypnosis. Adults may have preconceived notions or fears that can block the process, while children are more likely to approach hypnosis with curiosity and trust, making it easier for therapists to guide them into a trance-like state.

Benefits of Hypnosis for Children

Hypnosis can offer significant benefits for children, particularly when traditional forms of therapy or treatment may be less effective or difficult for them to engage in. Some of the conditions that hypnosis can address in children include:

- **Anxiety and Stress:** Children often face various stressors, such as school pressures, social challenges, and family issues. Hypnosis can help them manage anxiety by teaching relaxation techniques, focusing on positive imagery, and encouraging self-confidence. Guided relaxation can also help them to learn to cope with stressful situations, like school exams or public speaking.
- **Sleep Disorders:** Many children experience difficulties with sleep, such as insomnia, nightmares, or night terrors. Hypnosis can promote deep relaxation and help children develop healthier sleep patterns by guiding them to visualize calm, peaceful imagery before bed. Through hypnosis, children can also learn to reframe frightening thoughts or negative associations with sleep.

- **Behavioral Issues:** Hypnosis can be helpful in managing behavioral issues, including attention problems, impulsivity, and even bed-wetting. By focusing on the subconscious mind, hypnosis can help reprogram certain habits or thought patterns, making it easier for children to adopt healthier behaviors. It can also promote positive reinforcement for good behavior, helping to instill a sense of self-control.
- **Pain Management:** Children who experience chronic pain, such as from headaches or medical procedures, can benefit from hypnosis as a way to manage discomfort. Through visualization and relaxation, hypnosis can reduce the perception of pain and increase a child's tolerance for it. This is especially valuable in medical settings, where children may need to undergo procedures or treatments that can be distressing.
- **Phobias and Fears:** Hypnosis has been shown to help children overcome specific phobias, such as a fear of the dark, fear of animals, or separation anxiety. By guiding a child through a process of desensitization and introducing new, positive associations, hypnosis can reduce the emotional intensity of their fears and allow them to feel more comfortable in formerly distressing situations.

The Process of Hypnosis for Children

The process of hypnosis with children typically begins by establishing a safe, comfortable environment where the child feels at ease. This often includes using a calm and gentle tone, creating a non-threatening atmosphere, and engaging in age-appropriate language. For younger children, the therapist may incorporate playful elements, such as storytelling or games, to make the process more engaging and relatable.

The hypnotherapist will then guide the child into a relaxed state, often through visualization or deep breathing exercises. Depending on the child's age, the therapist might use metaphors or simple imagery, such as imagining floating on a cloud or walking through a peaceful garden, to deepen the child's relaxation and focus.

Once the child is deeply relaxed, the hypnotherapist can begin offering positive suggestions that are aligned with the child's goals. These suggestions might involve encouraging self-esteem, promoting relaxation, or reframing negative thoughts about specific fears or anxieties. The language used in these suggestions is carefully chosen to resonate with the child's understanding and emotional state.

For example, a therapist might suggest to a child experiencing anxiety about school, "You can feel calm and confident when you walk into the classroom because you know you have everything you need inside you to do your best."

While hypnosis can be an effective tool for helping children, it is essential to approach it with care and consideration. Here are some important points to keep in mind when using hypnosis with children:

- **Parental Involvement:** It is vital that parents or guardians are involved in the process, both for consent and support. Parental permission is typically required before any therapeutic work with a child begins, and it is helpful for parents to be aware of the goals and techniques involved. Parents can also play a role in reinforcing the positive suggestions and strategies learned during hypnosis in everyday situations.
- **Age Appropriateness:** The approach to hypnosis must be age-appropriate. Younger children, for example, may respond better to stories and metaphors, while older children may be able to engage more directly with the process and understand the rationale behind the techniques. The therapist should adjust their methods based on the child's developmental level to ensure the process is effective and comfortable.
- **Emotional Sensitivity:** Children can be more emotionally sensitive than adults, so the therapist must be mindful of the child's emotional state during hypnosis. If the child becomes distressed, the therapist should be prepared to ease them back into a state of calm. Hypnosis should never be used to push a child too far emotionally or to uncover traumatic memories without appropriate support.
- **Parental Expectations:** It's important to manage the expectations of parents, as they may be eager for quick results. Hypnosis is not a "magic fix" and may require multiple sessions to achieve lasting change. The therapist should emphasize the need for patience and consistency, as well as the importance of combining hypnosis with other forms of treatment when necessary.

While hypnosis can be a powerful tool, it is not always effective for every child or every issue. Some children may be less responsive to hypnosis due to factors like severe resistance, fear, or anxiety about the process. In these cases, the therapist may need to take a more gradual approach or explore alternative therapeutic techniques.

Additionally, hypnotherapy is not a substitute for traditional medical or psychological care. For children with severe mental health conditions or chronic physical illnesses, hypnosis should be considered as a complementary therapy rather than a primary treatment. It is essential for hypnotherapists to work alongside other healthcare providers to ensure the child is receiving comprehensive care.

Conclusion

Hypnosis offers a safe, non-invasive way to help children manage a variety of challenges, from emotional difficulties and behavioral issues to physical pain. When conducted by a trained and experienced hypnotherapist, it can empower children to make positive changes, improve their coping skills, and lead more fulfilling lives. By carefully considering the child's needs, age, and emotional state, hypnosis can be a valuable therapeutic tool that complements other forms of treatment and promotes lasting change.

Hypnosis as a Therapeutic Tool for Children

Hypnosis has gained recognition as a valuable therapeutic tool for addressing a wide range of issues in both adults and children. In pediatric care, hypnosis has proven to be particularly effective due to children's heightened imagination and suggestibility, which make them more receptive to therapeutic techniques that involve visualization, relaxation, and subconscious programming.

How Hypnosis Works with Children

Hypnosis for children is not about controlling or manipulating them but rather guiding them into a state of focused relaxation where they are more open to positive suggestions and constructive change. Children are naturally more imaginative and open to fantasy, which makes them ideal candidates for hypnotic interventions. This increased suggestibility allows the therapist to work with the child's subconscious mind to address issues ranging from anxiety to pain management and behavior modification.

The process typically begins with the child getting comfortable in a safe and quiet environment. The therapist uses a calm, soothing tone to help the child relax, often guiding them through breathing exercises or visualizations. These techniques can help the child enter a trance-like state, where their mind is deeply focused yet relaxed. In this state, the therapist can introduce positive affirmations or suggestions tailored to the child's specific needs.

Common Conditions Treated with Hypnosis in Children

Several emotional, psychological, and physical conditions can benefit from hypnosis, making it an effective tool for parents and pediatric professionals looking for non-invasive, supportive therapies for children. Some common areas where hypnosis has been shown to help children include:

- **Anxiety and Stress:** Many children experience stress due to school pressures, social situations, or family dynamics. Hypnosis helps reduce anxiety by teaching relaxation techniques and providing positive, calming imagery. For example, a child who is nervous about school presentations might be guided to visualize themselves performing confidently and calmly, helping to build self-assurance and reduce worry.

- **Sleep Disorders:** Sleep disturbances such as insomnia, nightmares, and night terrors are common in children. Hypnosis can help by introducing soothing thoughts and creating positive associations with bedtime. Through relaxation techniques and calming visualizations, children can overcome fears related to sleep and develop healthier sleep patterns.
- **Behavioral Issues:** Hypnosis can be a helpful intervention for children who struggle with behavioral problems such as hyperactivity, impulsivity, or aggression. By accessing the subconscious mind, hypnotherapists can encourage the child to adopt more appropriate behaviors, reinforcing positive actions and attitudes. The therapist might suggest ways for the child to feel more in control or develop patience in difficult situations.
- **Chronic Pain and Physical Discomfort:** Children with chronic conditions such as migraines, stomachaches, or pain due to injury can benefit from hypnosis as a complementary therapy for pain management. Hypnosis can help reduce the perception of pain, ease physical tension, and encourage the mind-body connection to promote healing. It's particularly useful in medical settings, where children may experience anxiety or discomfort during medical procedures or treatments.
- **Phobias and Fears:** Children often develop specific fears, such as a fear of the dark, insects, or separation anxiety. Hypnosis works by helping the child reframe their fears through gradual desensitization and visualization. For instance, a child afraid of the dark might be guided to imagine a comforting, peaceful place that is safe and full of light. With repeated sessions, the fear response is reduced, and the child can begin to face their fears more confidently.
- **Nail-biting and Other Habits:** Many children engage in habits such as nail-biting, thumb-sucking, or hair-pulling. Hypnosis can break these habitual behaviors by encouraging the subconscious mind to develop healthier alternatives. Through positive suggestions and reinforcement, children can learn to replace these habits with more productive behaviors.

Techniques Used in Pediatric Hypnosis

When working with children, therapists often adjust their approach to match the child's age, developmental stage, and preferences. Hypnosis techniques that work with adults might be simplified or made more engaging for younger patients. Some common methods used in pediatric hypnosis include:

- **Storytelling and Imagery:** Stories and metaphors are often used to make hypnosis more accessible and fun for children. A child might be asked to imagine themselves as a superhero, using their mind to control their body's responses, or to envision a magical place where they can feel calm and safe. These stories can help children visualize themselves overcoming challenges, whether it's calming their nerves before a test or reducing physical pain.

- **Progressive Relaxation:** One of the core techniques in hypnosis involves guiding the child through progressive muscle relaxation. The therapist may suggest that the child tense and then relax each part of their body, starting from their toes and moving up to their head. This helps release physical tension and calms the mind, preparing the child for deeper relaxation.
- **Visualization and Positive Affirmations:** Children can be taught to use their imagination to create positive, empowering mental images. For example, if a child struggles with anxiety, they may be guided to imagine themselves walking into a classroom with confidence, surrounded by positive energy. Positive affirmations may be used alongside visualization to reinforce feelings of calm, self-assurance, and control.

Safety and Ethical Considerations

Hypnosis is a safe, non-invasive therapy when conducted by a trained and certified hypnotherapist. However, like any therapeutic approach, it requires careful attention to ethical considerations. The child's safety, emotional well-being, and consent should always be the top priority. It is important for parents to be actively involved in the process, providing consent and reinforcing the work done during hypnosis. In many cases, the therapist will explain the process to both the child and their parents to ensure that they feel comfortable with the approach.

Hypnosis should never be used as a substitute for other medical or psychological interventions. It works best when integrated into a broader treatment plan that includes traditional therapies, such as cognitive-behavioral therapy (CBT) or medical care for physical conditions. If a child has a history of trauma or deep psychological issues, hypnosis should be used with caution and in conjunction with a licensed mental health professional.

Conclusion

Hypnosis offers a safe and effective therapeutic option for children, addressing a wide range of emotional, behavioral, and physical challenges. By leveraging the power of the subconscious mind, hypnosis helps children manage anxiety, stress, phobias, and habits, while also promoting healthier sleep patterns and pain management. The key to successful hypnosis with children lies in creating a comfortable, non-threatening environment where the child can feel empowered and in control of their own healing process. When used ethically and appropriately, hypnosis can be a powerful tool for helping children lead healthier, happier lives.

Case Studies

Case studies demonstrate the wide-ranging effectiveness of hypnosis in addressing various conditions in both children and adults. These real-life examples provide insight into how hypnosis can be applied therapeutically and the positive outcomes that can result when used appropriately. Here are a few notable cases where hypnosis was instrumental in improving a patient's well-being:

Case Study 1: Managing Childhood Anxiety

A 10-year-old boy named Ethan had been struggling with severe anxiety, particularly around school presentations. He would experience panic attacks, often resulting in avoidance of school activities. His parents sought hypnosis as a complementary treatment alongside traditional counseling. Through a series of sessions, the hypnotherapist used guided imagery and progressive relaxation techniques, helping Ethan visualize himself confidently speaking in front of the class. After just a few sessions, Ethan began to feel more relaxed and calm before presentations, and his anxiety reduced significantly. Within a few months, he was able to speak in front of his class with ease, a dramatic improvement from his initial struggle.

Case Study 2: Overcoming Bed-Wetting in a Child

Sarah, an 8-year-old girl, had been dealing with nighttime bed-wetting for several years. Despite medical evaluations showing no underlying physical cause, her parents were frustrated with the lack of progress. After consulting a hypnotherapist, Sarah began weekly sessions aimed at addressing her subconscious fear of being separated from her parents at night. Through relaxation techniques and suggestions for better bladder control, Sarah learned to associate nighttime with relaxation and confidence. After several months of hypnosis, Sarah's bed-wetting episodes significantly decreased, and she eventually stopped wetting the bed altogether. This case highlighted how hypnosis could help modify subconscious patterns tied to emotional stress.

Case Study 3: Pain Management in a Teenager

Mark, a 16-year-old teenager, had been experiencing chronic migraines for over a year. Conventional treatments, including medication and lifestyle changes, had not provided much relief. After a comprehensive assessment, his doctor recommended hypnosis as an alternative treatment. In Mark's case, hypnosis was used to help reduce the frequency and intensity of his migraines by teaching him how to use relaxation techniques and self-hypnosis. The hypnotherapist guided Mark through visualization exercises, where he would imagine his body relaxing and the pain dissipating with each breath. After a few weeks of sessions, Mark reported a significant reduction in both the number and severity of his headaches, and he was able to manage his migraines more effectively.

Case Study 4: Smoking Cessation in an Adult

Maria, a 34-year-old woman, had been smoking for over 15 years and had tried various methods to quit, including patches, gum, and behavioral therapy, but none had been successful. After hearing about hypnosis for smoking cessation, Maria decided to give it a try. During her hypnotherapy sessions, the therapist focused on changing her mindset towards smoking by using post-hypnotic suggestions that reinforced her desire to quit and associated smoking with negative emotions. Over the course of several sessions, Maria reported a decrease in cravings and a growing sense of control over her behavior. After completing the treatment, Maria successfully quit smoking and remained smoke-free for over a year. This case highlighted the power of hypnosis in overcoming deeply ingrained habits.

Case Study 5: Weight Loss and Hypnosis

Tom, a 45-year-old man, had struggled with overeating and weight gain for years. Despite various diets and exercise programs, he was unable to sustain long-term weight loss. His hypnotherapist used cognitive behavioral hypnosis techniques to identify the underlying emotional triggers for his overeating habits. Through a series of sessions, Tom was able to reprogram his subconscious mind to view food differently, focusing on healthy eating habits and recognizing emotional triggers without resorting to food. As a result, Tom began making healthier choices, losing weight steadily, and feeling more in control of his eating habits. Over six months, he lost over 30 pounds and continued to maintain his weight loss.

Case Study 6: Phobia Treatment in a Young Adult

Jane, a 25-year-old woman, had a debilitating fear of flying that had prevented her from traveling for years. Despite understanding that her fear was irrational, Jane could not overcome the anxiety she felt before and during flights. After a few sessions with a hypnotherapist, Jane was guided through a process of deep relaxation and positive suggestions. During hypnosis, she was asked to imagine herself flying comfortably and calmly, visualizing each step of the journey from takeoff to landing. As the sessions progressed, Jane reported a decrease in her anxiety and was able to board a flight for the first time in over five years. This case demonstrated how hypnosis could be used to address phobias and fears by reprogramming the mind to respond calmly to triggers.

David, a 40-year-old executive, had been experiencing high levels of stress due to his demanding job and long hours. His stress was affecting his personal relationships and overall health, including frequent tension headaches. Through hypnosis, David was able to learn relaxation techniques that helped him manage stress more effectively. The hypnotherapist guided him to visualize a peaceful, serene place whenever he felt overwhelmed, allowing David to de-stress quickly and gain better control over his emotions. Over several sessions, David felt more balanced and was able to reduce his stress levels significantly, improving both his work performance and quality of life.

Conclusion

These case studies highlight the versatility and effectiveness of hypnosis in treating a variety of conditions, from anxiety and pain management to phobias and smoking cessation. Hypnosis provides a powerful tool for accessing the subconscious mind and making lasting, positive changes. While individual experiences with hypnosis may vary, these cases underscore the potential benefits of this therapeutic technique in addressing both physical and emotional challenges. With the right approach, hypnosis can be an effective solution for many seeking relief from difficult conditions.

Hypnosis in Modern Medicine

In modern medicine, hypnosis has gained recognition as a complementary therapeutic tool, used to treat a variety of conditions, from chronic pain to psychological disorders. Once viewed with skepticism, it has gradually evolved into a respected practice within both medical and psychological settings, often used alongside conventional treatments to enhance patient outcomes.

One of the most significant areas where hypnosis has found a place in modern medicine is pain management. Research has shown that hypnotic techniques can significantly reduce the perception of pain, making it particularly useful for patients undergoing surgery, those with chronic pain conditions like fibromyalgia or arthritis, and individuals receiving cancer treatments. Studies have found that hypnosis can lower the need for anesthesia during certain procedures and reduce post-operative discomfort. By guiding patients into a deeply relaxed state, hypnosis allows them to focus their minds away from pain and stress, facilitating natural pain relief.

Hypnosis has also become an adjunctive treatment in the management of anxiety and stress-related conditions. Patients with anxiety disorders, post-traumatic stress disorder (PTSD), and insomnia often experience improvements with hypnotherapy. By addressing the root causes of stress and helping patients reframe negative thought patterns, hypnosis can help regulate the body's stress response, lowering cortisol levels and promoting a sense of calm. Additionally, individuals with high blood pressure have been found to benefit from hypnosis, as it can assist in reducing both physical tension and mental stress, potentially leading to lower blood pressure readings.

In the realm of mental health, hypnosis has proven effective in treating conditions such as depression, phobias, and addiction. Hypnotherapy works by accessing the subconscious mind, where deeply rooted beliefs and behaviors can be modified. It can be particularly effective in helping individuals overcome habits like smoking, overeating, or alcohol abuse. By reinforcing positive behavior through post-hypnotic suggestions, patients can develop healthier coping mechanisms and break free from harmful patterns.

Another growing application of hypnosis in modern medicine is in the field of gastrointestinal disorders. Conditions like irritable bowel syndrome (IBS), acid reflux, and even chronic constipation have shown improvement with the use of hypnosis. Studies have demonstrated that hypnosis can influence the autonomic nervous system, leading to reduced symptoms of gastrointestinal distress. By addressing emotional triggers and enhancing relaxation, patients with IBS, for example, have reported fewer flare-ups and a better overall quality of life.

Hypnosis is also gaining traction in pediatric care, particularly in the treatment of children with anxiety, pain, and behavioral issues. Pediatric hypnosis is often used in a playful, age-appropriate way to engage children, helping them manage symptoms of conditions like asthma, headaches, or even in preparation for medical procedures. Research has shown that children can respond particularly well to hypnosis, as they have a highly imaginative and suggestible nature, making them more open to the process.

While the evidence supporting hypnosis continues to grow, it is important to note that it is not a one-size-fits-all solution. Hypnosis works best for individuals who are receptive to suggestion and willing to participate in the process. It should always be conducted by trained professionals, particularly in medical settings, where its use requires careful consideration and expertise.

In summary, hypnosis has firmly established its place in modern medicine, offering a non-invasive, drug-free approach to treating a wide range of conditions. Whether used to manage pain, reduce stress, treat psychological disorders, or aid in behavioral change, hypnosis provides a valuable tool for enhancing traditional medical treatments. As research continues to explore its potential, the integration of hypnosis into mainstream medical practice may offer even more benefits for patients seeking holistic, effective care.

Hypnosis as a Complementary Treatment

Hypnosis is increasingly being recognized as a valuable complementary treatment alongside conventional medical and psychological therapies. Rather than replacing standard care, hypnosis works synergistically with traditional treatments, helping to enhance their effectiveness and providing patients with additional tools for managing various conditions.

One of the primary areas where hypnosis has shown significant promise is in pain management. For individuals undergoing surgery, those with chronic pain conditions, or patients receiving chemotherapy, hypnosis can reduce the perception of pain and help manage discomfort. This is particularly beneficial for patients who may wish to reduce their reliance on pharmaceutical painkillers, potentially minimizing the risk of side effects or addiction. By inducing a deeply relaxed state and guiding patients to focus on positive imagery and sensations, hypnosis helps alter the brain's response to pain, making it less intense and more manageable.

Another area where hypnosis is used as a complementary treatment is in mental health care, particularly in addressing anxiety, depression, and stress-related disorders. Hypnosis can help patients manage the emotional and psychological components of these conditions by promoting relaxation, enhancing self-awareness, and encouraging positive behavioral changes. For example, in cases of anxiety or PTSD, hypnosis can assist patients in confronting and processing past traumatic experiences in a safe, controlled environment, often leading to a reduction in symptoms. Additionally, hypnotherapy can help individuals overcome destructive thought patterns and develop healthier coping strategies, working in tandem with other therapeutic approaches such as cognitive-behavioral therapy (CBT) or medication.

Hypnosis also complements treatments for addiction, including smoking cessation and weight loss programs. Many addiction treatment programs incorporate hypnosis to help patients address the subconscious triggers that fuel their cravings and unhealthy habits. For example, individuals trying to quit smoking may undergo hypnosis to strengthen their motivation, reframe their relationship with tobacco, and reduce withdrawal symptoms. Likewise, hypnosis can be an effective tool in weight loss programs, helping patients address emotional eating, reduce cravings, and improve self-control.

In the field of gastrointestinal health, hypnosis is increasingly being used to treat conditions like irritable bowel syndrome (IBS), acid reflux, and chronic constipation. Studies have shown that hypnosis can help regulate the autonomic nervous system, which controls digestive processes. By reducing stress and promoting relaxation, hypnosis has been shown to alleviate symptoms of IBS and other digestive disorders, often providing relief when traditional treatments have not been fully effective.

In addition to these specific conditions, hypnosis is frequently used to help patients manage symptoms associated with chronic illnesses or procedures. For example, it has been successfully used in oncology to help patients manage pain, reduce nausea from chemotherapy, and improve their overall sense of well-being. Similarly, hypnosis has been shown to help patients with sleep disorders, fibromyalgia, and headaches by addressing the underlying psychological and physiological factors contributing to these conditions.

Though hypnosis can be highly effective as a complementary treatment, it is important to remember that it is most beneficial when used alongside, not instead of, conventional medical care. For instance, hypnosis should not be seen as a substitute for surgery, essential medication, or other critical medical interventions. Rather, it should be viewed as an adjunctive therapy that can support the healing process and improve overall treatment outcomes.

The effectiveness of hypnosis as a complementary treatment also depends on the individual's willingness and receptivity to the process. While some individuals are highly responsive to hypnosis, others may be less susceptible to its effects. Therefore, it is crucial for both practitioners and patients to establish realistic expectations for the role hypnosis will play in the treatment plan.

As research continues to explore the therapeutic potential of hypnosis, its role in modern medicine will likely expand. Its non-invasive nature, minimal side effects, and ability to complement traditional therapies make hypnosis an increasingly valuable option for individuals seeking holistic and integrative approaches to health and well-being. By working alongside conventional treatments, hypnosis can help patients achieve more comprehensive, well-rounded care, addressing both the physical and psychological aspects of their health.

Hypnosis in Surgery

Hypnosis has increasingly been explored as a viable option in the realm of surgery, offering patients a non-pharmacological alternative for pain management, anxiety reduction, and even enhancing the overall surgical experience. While it is not meant to replace anesthesia entirely in major procedures, the use of hypnosis in surgery provides an innovative way to support the patient's body and mind during the process.

One of the key benefits of using hypnosis in surgery is its ability to reduce the need for anesthetic drugs, particularly in minor procedures. Hypnosis can help patients enter a deeply relaxed, trance-like state where they are more focused and less sensitive to pain. During this state, patients often report feeling detached from their body, which allows them to endure surgical procedures with little to no discomfort. This can be particularly useful for those who cannot tolerate certain medications due to allergies, adverse reactions, or personal preferences, offering a drug-free option for pain relief.

In addition to pain management, hypnosis is also effective in alleviating pre-surgery anxiety and stress. The anticipation of surgery can cause significant emotional distress, leading to elevated blood pressure, increased heart rate, and heightened feelings of fear. Hypnosis can help calm the nervous system by encouraging deep relaxation and guiding patients through calming visualizations. By addressing these anxieties, hypnosis not only improves the emotional experience of the patient but also helps optimize the body's physical response to the surgical procedure, promoting a smoother recovery.

Post-operative recovery is another area where hypnosis can be beneficial. After surgery, patients often experience anxiety, nausea, or difficulty coping with the recovery process. Hypnotherapy can aid in the post-surgical healing process by promoting relaxation, reducing stress, and even addressing issues like sleep disturbances or nausea related to anesthesia. In some cases, hypnosis has been shown to reduce the need for pain medication during the recovery phase, which can speed up recovery and reduce the risk of side effects associated with pharmaceuticals.

There is growing evidence that hypnosis can support a faster recovery by reducing complications such as excessive bleeding, prolonged swelling, or wound healing delays. Studies have indicated that patients who undergo hypnosis prior to surgery may experience a more rapid healing process, likely due to the reduced stress levels and improved immune function associated with relaxation techniques.

Although hypnosis is not suitable for all surgical cases, it has been shown to be particularly effective in procedures such as dental surgery, skin grafts, biopsies, and even more complex operations like caesarean sections and joint replacement surgeries. In these cases, hypnosis is typically used as part of a multi-disciplinary approach, working alongside standard anesthesia and pain management protocols.

The technique itself involves the patient working closely with a trained hypnotherapist, who uses guided imagery, verbal suggestions, and relaxation techniques to bring the patient into a highly focused state. While under hypnosis, the patient may be instructed to visualize a calm and peaceful setting or focus on specific physical sensations that promote healing. The hypnotherapist can also provide suggestions for pain reduction and emotional calming to help the patient feel more comfortable during the procedure.

The benefits of using hypnosis in surgery extend beyond the physical and psychological aspects of the experience. For medical professionals, incorporating hypnosis into the surgical process can lead to greater patient satisfaction, smoother procedures, and possibly reduced recovery times. It also provides a valuable option for patients who seek a more holistic approach to surgery, allowing them to feel more in control of their experience.

Despite its advantages, the use of hypnosis in surgery is still relatively underutilized and requires more research to fully understand its capabilities and limitations. It is important for patients and medical practitioners to have clear communication regarding the use of hypnosis, ensuring that it is employed appropriately as a complement to traditional medical practices.

Overall, hypnosis in surgery represents an exciting frontier in medical care, offering patients a natural, non-invasive method to enhance the surgical experience. By addressing pain, anxiety, and post-operative recovery, hypnosis can contribute to a more holistic, patient-centered approach to surgery that supports both physical and emotional well-being.

Research on Medical Hypnosis

Research on the use of hypnosis in medicine has expanded over the past few decades, uncovering its potential as an effective complementary treatment for a wide range of physical and psychological conditions. Studies have consistently demonstrated that hypnosis can be a powerful tool in managing pain, reducing anxiety, and improving overall patient outcomes.

One of the most extensively researched areas of medical hypnosis is pain management. Numerous studies have shown that hypnosis can significantly reduce the perception of pain in patients undergoing surgery, chronic pain conditions, and cancer treatments. For instance, research has highlighted that patients who underwent hypnosis before and during surgery reported lower levels of pain and required less post-operative analgesia compared to those who relied solely on conventional anesthesia. Studies in chronic pain management have also demonstrated that hypnosis can reduce the intensity of pain experienced by patients with conditions like fibromyalgia, arthritis, and migraine headaches. By utilizing relaxation techniques and suggestion, hypnosis can alter the brain's perception of pain, making it less distressing for the patient.

In addition to its impact on pain, hypnosis has shown promise in reducing stress and anxiety, both before and after medical procedures. Research suggests that hypnosis can lower blood pressure, decrease heart rate, and promote a sense of calm in patients facing anxiety-inducing treatments such as surgery, dental work, or chemotherapy. A meta-analysis of studies on hypnosis for anxiety revealed that it can be a highly effective intervention for pre-operative anxiety and post-operative recovery, particularly in reducing the emotional distress that often accompanies medical procedures. By guiding patients into a deeply relaxed state, hypnosis helps mitigate the physiological stress response, improving the overall experience of the patient.

Hypnosis has also been investigated for its potential in managing conditions related to the gastrointestinal system. Conditions such as irritable bowel syndrome (IBS), acid reflux, and chronic constipation have shown improvement through the use of hypnosis. Research in this area suggests that hypnosis can influence the autonomic nervous system, which controls digestive processes, by reducing stress and promoting relaxation. A study on IBS patients found that those who underwent hypnotherapy experienced a significant reduction in symptoms, including abdominal pain, bloating, and irregular bowel movements, compared to those receiving standard treatments. The mind-body connection plays a crucial role in gastrointestinal health, and hypnosis can help patients regain balance in both their physical and emotional states.

In the realm of addiction treatment, hypnosis has been explored as a tool for helping individuals overcome habits like smoking, overeating, and alcohol dependence. Studies have indicated that hypnosis can help change the subconscious patterns that contribute to these behaviors, making it easier for individuals to break free from unhealthy habits. Research on smoking cessation, for example, shows that hypnotherapy can significantly increase the success rate for quitting smoking, especially when combined with other therapeutic techniques. Hypnosis works by reinforcing positive behaviors and offering suggestions that help patients replace cravings with healthier alternatives.

Hypnosis is also gaining traction in the field of oncology, where it has been used to reduce nausea and vomiting caused by chemotherapy, alleviate pain, and manage the emotional challenges faced by cancer patients. A number of studies have found that cancer patients who received hypnosis reported a greater sense of control, reduced pain, and fewer chemotherapy-related side effects. By tapping into the subconscious mind, hypnosis offers a non-invasive and drug-free way to support patients during their treatment journey.

Additionally, there is growing interest in the use of hypnosis for sleep disorders, such as insomnia, and for enhancing cognitive performance in patients recovering from surgery or trauma. Research has shown that hypnosis can improve sleep quality by helping patients manage stress and anxiety, which are often key contributors to insomnia. In terms of cognitive recovery, hypnosis has been found to assist patients in regaining mental clarity, focus, and overall well-being following major medical procedures.

While the research on medical hypnosis is promising, there is still much to learn about its full potential and the mechanisms behind its effectiveness. Most studies suggest that hypnosis works best in combination with other forms of treatment, rather than as a standalone therapy. It is also important to recognize that not all individuals are equally responsive to hypnosis, and its success depends on the person's susceptibility to suggestion and their willingness to participate in the process.

In summary, research on medical hypnosis has consistently demonstrated its value in managing pain, reducing stress and anxiety, improving recovery outcomes, and supporting behavioral change. As studies continue to explore its various applications, it is likely that hypnosis will play an increasingly important role in integrative medicine, offering patients a holistic, non-invasive approach to improving their health and well-being. The growing body of evidence supporting hypnosis as a therapeutic tool underscores its potential to enhance traditional medical treatments and provide patients with a deeper sense of control over their healing process.

Negative Aspects of Hypnosis

While hypnosis has gained recognition for its therapeutic benefits, it is not without potential drawbacks and limitations. Like any medical or psychological technique, it carries risks, especially when not used properly or when applied inappropriately. Understanding these negative aspects is crucial for both practitioners and patients to make informed decisions about its use.

One of the primary concerns with hypnosis is the potential for misuse. When performed by an unqualified or inexperienced practitioner, hypnosis can lead to unintended or harmful effects. For instance, poorly conducted hypnosis sessions may create false memories or "suggested" memories, a phenomenon known as *false memory syndrome.* This is particularly problematic in situations where individuals are guided into believing they have experienced events that never actually occurred. False memories can be damaging, especially in therapeutic contexts where the individual may be encouraged to revisit traumatic events that never happened, leading to unnecessary emotional distress or confusion.

Additionally, hypnosis requires a certain level of suggestibility from the individual, which means not everyone is equally susceptible to it. While some people can easily enter a hypnotic state, others may find it difficult or impossible to do so. Individuals who are resistant to hypnosis may not experience the intended benefits, which can lead to frustration or disappointment. This variability in susceptibility makes it less reliable than other treatment methods for some people.

Hypnosis also carries the risk of exacerbating existing psychological issues. For individuals with certain mental health conditions, such as dissociative disorders, hypnosis may trigger adverse reactions. These individuals may experience episodes of dissociation or feel disconnected from their sense of self, which can deepen feelings of distress or confusion. In some rare cases, people with severe psychological conditions like borderline personality disorder or psychosis might find that hypnosis leads to the surfacing of repressed memories or emotions that they are not equipped to handle. For these individuals, the experience could intensify feelings of fear or helplessness rather than promote healing.

There is also the potential for hypnosis to be used inappropriately for entertainment purposes. Stage hypnosis, for example, is often seen in entertainment settings where the performer encourages participants to engage in comedic or bizarre behavior while under hypnosis. While harmless in most cases, stage hypnosis can perpetuate misconceptions about the technique, leading people to believe it is merely a form of mind control or that individuals can be coerced into actions against their will. This can undermine the seriousness with which hypnosis is regarded in therapeutic settings and may make some people wary of its use in a clinical context.

Another consideration is the possibility of dependency. Some individuals may come to rely on hypnosis as a crutch for managing anxiety, pain, or other issues, potentially avoiding addressing the underlying causes of their problems. Hypnosis is generally most effective when used as part of a broader treatment plan, but if overused or relied upon too heavily, it may delay other necessary therapeutic interventions. This can prevent individuals from engaging in the deeper work needed for lasting behavioral or psychological change.

Finally, there is a lack of standardization and regulation within the field of hypnosis. While clinical hypnosis is practiced by trained professionals, such as licensed therapists and psychologists, the practice is not always regulated in the same way as other forms of therapy. This means that anyone, regardless of qualifications, could advertise themselves as a "hypnotherapist." This lack of oversight increases the risk of encountering individuals who lack the necessary skills or knowledge to conduct hypnosis safely and effectively. Without proper training, some practitioners may make unrealistic promises or use techniques that could potentially harm rather than help the client.

In summary, while hypnosis has proven to be a valuable tool in many therapeutic contexts, it is not without its negative aspects. Misuse, the risk of false memories, varying levels of susceptibility, potential exacerbation of mental health conditions, dependency, and the lack of standardization all pose challenges to its widespread acceptance and use. It is essential for individuals considering hypnosis as a treatment option to seek a qualified, experienced practitioner and to use hypnosis as part of a comprehensive, well-rounded approach to healing and personal growth.

Misuse of Hypnosis

Misuse of hypnosis can occur in various ways, and its potential for harm is a significant concern, especially when the technique is applied improperly or by unqualified practitioners. While hypnosis itself is generally a safe and effective tool when used in the right context, its misuse can lead to emotional distress, false memories, and in some cases, exploitation of vulnerable individuals.

One of the most notable risks of misuse is the creation of false memories, also known as *memory distortion* or *false memory syndrome*. Under hypnosis, a person is highly suggestible, which means that suggestions made by a therapist, intentionally or unintentionally, can alter their recollection of past events. This is particularly problematic in legal or therapeutic settings where individuals might be encouraged to "remember" traumatic events that never happened. In cases of repressed memory recovery, for example, the hypnotist might inadvertently plant memories of abuse or trauma that were not part of the person's actual history, leading to confusion, distress, and even legal consequences. While rare, false memories can be deeply damaging, especially if the person believes in the fabricated memories as true.

Another form of misuse occurs in unethical or exploitative situations, such as in stage hypnosis or entertainment. While typically seen as harmless fun, stage hypnosis can distort public perception of the technique, making it seem like a form of mind control. In some cases, participants may be encouraged to perform embarrassing or unsafe actions while under hypnosis, which can lead to emotional or psychological harm. This trivializes hypnosis and gives the false impression that it can control a person's actions against their will, further stigmatizing its therapeutic potential.

Hypnosis can also be misused when practiced by individuals without proper training or certification. A person who lacks formal education in hypnosis may attempt to use the technique on vulnerable individuals, leading to harmful or ineffective treatment. Inadequate knowledge of the subconscious mind and the complex dynamics of suggestion can result in inappropriate or harmful interventions. For example, an untrained hypnotist might attempt to address issues that require medical or psychological treatment, such as severe anxiety, depression, or trauma, without recognizing the need for additional therapeutic modalities. This can delay appropriate care, exacerbate the person's condition, or even cause further harm.

The ethical risks of misuse are particularly significant in the context of vulnerable populations. People seeking hypnosis for stress management, pain relief, or behavioral change may be at a heightened state of emotional or psychological need, making them more susceptible to the influence of an unscrupulous practitioner. In some cases, individuals may be taken advantage of by therapists or hypnotherapists who make exaggerated claims about the effectiveness of hypnosis or who pressure clients into extended treatments that are unnecessary or overly costly. This not only undermines the integrity of the therapy but can also cause financial or emotional harm to the individual.

Furthermore, hypnosis can be misused to manipulate or control people in personal or professional relationships. In rare cases, individuals might attempt to use hypnosis for coercive purposes, attempting to influence others' decisions, thoughts, or actions without their consent. While hypnosis cannot truly control a person's will in the way it is often portrayed in movies, it can still be used to exploit people's suggestibility, leading to potential abuse of power. This is why ethical guidelines and professional standards are crucial in any practice involving hypnosis.

In clinical settings, another misuse of hypnosis is to apply it as a sole treatment for conditions that require comprehensive, multi-faceted care. For instance, hypnosis may be useful in managing pain or reducing anxiety, but it is unlikely to be sufficient for treating serious mental health issues like schizophrenia, bipolar disorder, or severe depression. Relying exclusively on hypnosis for such conditions can delay access to the proper treatment, such as medication or psychotherapy, and result in worsening of the individual's condition.

Lastly, misuse of hypnosis can also occur when it is used inappropriately during medical procedures. While hypnosis has been shown to assist with pain management in certain cases, it should not replace necessary medical interventions, especially in emergency or surgical situations. Using hypnosis as a primary anesthesia or sedation method without adequate medical supervision can pose serious risks, including unaddressed medical conditions or complications that may require immediate attention.

In conclusion, while hypnosis is a powerful and beneficial tool when applied correctly, its misuse can lead to significant harm, including false memories, exploitation, delayed medical treatment, and emotional distress. It is crucial for both practitioners and clients to recognize the ethical boundaries of hypnosis and to ensure that it is used only by trained, certified professionals in appropriate contexts. Establishing ethical guidelines and ensuring that hypnosis is conducted with care and integrity are essential steps in preventing misuse and maximizing its therapeutic potential.

Potential Risks of Hypnosis

While hypnosis can be a valuable therapeutic tool, it is important to acknowledge that it comes with potential risks. Though generally safe when performed by trained professionals, there are circumstances where hypnosis may have unintended or harmful effects. Understanding these risks can help individuals make informed decisions about whether hypnosis is the right approach for them.

One of the key risks associated with hypnosis is the potential for memory distortion. During a hypnotic state, individuals are highly suggestible, and this heightened suggestibility can sometimes lead to false memories or confabulations. In some cases, a person might be led to believe they have experienced an event that never actually occurred. This is especially concerning in cases where hypnosis is used for memory recall, such as attempting to recover repressed memories. While these false memories may not be intentionally planted, the process of suggestion under hypnosis can sometimes distort the person's recollection of past events. This can be particularly problematic in legal settings or therapeutic environments where the accuracy of memories is critical.

Another risk of hypnosis lies in its potential to amplify existing mental health conditions. For individuals with certain psychological disorders, particularly those involving dissociation or trauma, hypnosis may inadvertently trigger emotional distress or worsen symptoms. For example, individuals with post-traumatic stress disorder (PTSD) may experience a reliving of traumatic memories under hypnosis, which can exacerbate feelings of fear, helplessness, or anxiety. Those with dissociative disorders may find themselves feeling disconnected from their sense of self, which can increase feelings of confusion or alienation.

In some cases, hypnosis can lead to an emotional or psychological "crisis" following a session. This is more likely to occur if the hypnotic process uncovers repressed emotions or unresolved trauma. While some individuals may find this cathartic or helpful, others may struggle to integrate these experiences, leading to distress or confusion in the days following the session. For this reason, it is important for practitioners to be cautious and prepared to offer support if such emotional reactions occur.

Additionally, there is the possibility of post-hypnotic suggestions causing unintended consequences. Post-hypnotic suggestions are instructions given to the subconscious mind during hypnosis, which the individual is meant to act upon after the session ends. If these suggestions are poorly phrased or not in alignment with the individual's true goals or values, they could lead to behaviors that the person does not consciously intend. This is why it is critical that suggestions made during hypnosis are clear, ethical, and tailored to the individual's needs.

Hypnosis also carries the risk of over-reliance. While hypnosis can be a powerful tool for managing certain conditions, such as stress, anxiety, or pain, it should not be considered a panacea. Over-reliance on hypnosis without addressing the underlying causes of the problem can lead to a temporary or superficial solution, preventing the person from engaging in more comprehensive, long-term therapies. For instance, using hypnosis as the sole treatment for serious mental health conditions, like depression or anxiety, without additional therapy or medication, may not provide the lasting results necessary for full recovery.

Another significant risk is the potential for exploitation. In the absence of proper training, individuals may use hypnosis in unethical or harmful ways. This is especially concerning in cases where the practitioner is not adequately trained or certified. Misuse can range from coercion or manipulation to creating false memories, leading to emotional harm for the individual. Furthermore, individuals with vulnerable psychological states, such as those seeking help for anxiety or trauma, may be more susceptible to the influence of an unqualified practitioner.

Finally, hypnosis may not be effective for everyone. While some individuals are highly susceptible to hypnotic suggestion, others may find it difficult or impossible to enter a hypnotic state. This variability in response can lead to disappointment or frustration for individuals who may have been hopeful about the potential benefits of hypnosis. Additionally, people with certain cognitive impairments or mental health conditions may find it challenging to benefit from hypnosis in the same way others do.

In conclusion, while hypnosis can be a beneficial and transformative tool in many therapeutic contexts, it is not without its risks. Memory distortion, exacerbation of mental health issues, emotional crises, post-hypnotic suggestion issues, over-reliance, exploitation, and variability in effectiveness all need to be considered before undergoing hypnosis. As with any therapeutic technique, hypnosis should be approached with caution, and individuals should ensure they are working with qualified, ethical practitioners who understand the complexities and limitations of the method. By being aware of these potential risks, clients can make better decisions about how to incorporate hypnosis into their overall wellness and healing journey.

Ethics in Hypnotherapy

Ethics in hypnotherapy is a crucial aspect of ensuring that the practice is used responsibly, with respect for the well-being and autonomy of clients. As a form of therapy that works with the subconscious mind, hypnotherapy can have a profound impact on a person's thoughts, emotions, and behaviors. Due to the sensitive nature of this work, hypnotherapists must adhere to a strict ethical framework to maintain trust, integrity, and professionalism in their practice.

One of the primary ethical considerations in hypnotherapy is the concept of informed consent. Before beginning any session, the hypnotherapist must ensure that the client fully understands the process, including the goals, methods, and potential risks involved. This involves explaining what hypnosis is, what the client can expect to experience during the session, and the therapeutic approach being used. Clients should feel free to ask questions and should be assured that they can withdraw consent at any time during the process. This empowers clients to make informed decisions about their participation, ensuring they are comfortable with the treatment.

Respecting client autonomy is another fundamental ethical principle in hypnotherapy. The hypnotist's role is to guide the client's subconscious mind, not to control or manipulate it. The client should never be made to do anything they do not want to do or that goes against their values and beliefs. A skilled hypnotherapist knows that hypnosis cannot be used for coercion or mind control. They must always maintain a professional distance and not use hypnosis for any form of manipulation, whether personal, financial, or otherwise.

Confidentiality is also essential in hypnotherapy. Like any form of therapy, the information shared between a client and hypnotherapist should remain confidential, with the exception of situations where there is a risk of harm to the client or others. The hypnotherapist must create a safe space where the client feels comfortable discussing deeply personal issues without fear of judgment or breach of privacy. This is particularly important in hypnotherapy, as the nature of the work may involve exploring repressed memories, traumatic experiences, or sensitive emotions.

Ethical hypnotherapists also recognize the limitations of their practice and are committed to referring clients to other professionals when necessary. Hypnotherapy is not a substitute for medical, psychiatric, or psychological treatment, and hypnotherapists must not attempt to diagnose or treat conditions outside the scope of their training. For example, if a client presents with severe mental health issues, such as schizophrenia or bipolar disorder, the hypnotherapist should refer them to a licensed mental health professional. Practitioners should avoid overstepping their boundaries, ensuring that clients receive comprehensive care that may involve a combination of therapies.

Another critical ethical consideration is the avoidance of false promises or claims about the effectiveness of hypnosis. Hypnotherapists must not guarantee results or offer unrealistic expectations. While hypnosis can be effective for various conditions, such as stress, anxiety, pain management, and behavioral change, it is not a cure-all. Clients should be made aware that results can vary, and no one should be led to believe that hypnosis will solve all of their problems or provide an instant fix. Clear communication about what hypnosis can and cannot do is necessary to prevent disappointment or the development of unrealistic hopes.

Hypnotherapists also have an ethical obligation to maintain their professional competence. This means staying up to date with the latest research, techniques, and best practices in the field. Continuing education and supervision are important components of ethical practice, ensuring that hypnotherapists are providing the most effective and evidence-based interventions. Practitioners should also be transparent about their qualifications, training, and experience, allowing clients to make informed choices about who they seek treatment from.

The issue of using hypnosis in vulnerable populations, such as children or those experiencing significant mental health challenges, requires particular attention. Special care must be taken to ensure that these individuals are treated with sensitivity and respect. In cases involving children, parental consent is essential, and the treatment should always be tailored to the child's developmental level. In cases where clients have a history of trauma, hypnotic techniques should be employed with caution to avoid retraumatization or emotional harm.

Lastly, hypnotherapists should be aware of the power dynamics inherent in the therapeutic relationship. Given that clients may be in a highly suggestible state during hypnosis, it is important for therapists to maintain an ethical balance of power. They must always act in the best interests of the client, avoiding any behavior that could exploit or harm them. This includes refraining from making suggestions that could be manipulative or that could lead to negative outcomes.

In conclusion, ethical practice in hypnotherapy is essential for ensuring the safety, well-being, and dignity of clients. By adhering to the principles of informed consent, respect for autonomy, confidentiality, professional competence, and transparency, hypnotherapists can build trusting and effective therapeutic relationships. Hypnosis has the potential to be a powerful and transformative tool, but it must be practiced with the

utmost care and responsibility to ensure that it benefits clients in a safe and respectful manner.

How hypnosis can increase your confidence

- Overcome self-doubt and build self-assurance.
- Improve public speaking skills and reduce nervousness.
- Boost performance in professional and personal settings.
- Strengthen self-belief in social interactions.
- Overcome the fear of rejection in social situations.
- Increase assertiveness in both personal and professional life.
- Build the courage to pursue new opportunities.
- Eliminate negative self-talk and replace it with empowering thoughts.
- Manage and reduce performance anxiety.
- Cultivate a positive mindset to tackle challenges with confidence.
- Improve self-image and develop a healthier relationship with oneself.
- Overcome feelings of inadequacy and feelings of not being good enough.
- Overcome fear of failure and embrace challenges with resilience.
- Help break free from the grip of perfectionism.
- Reduce fear of making mistakes and allow room for growth.
- Strengthen personal boundaries and assert your needs.
- Empower yourself to stand up for your values.
- Increase your ability to make decisions confidently.
- Overcome fear of judgment from others.
- Strengthen self-worth and self-respect.
- Develop a sense of control over your emotions and reactions.
- Build confidence in your abilities and skills.
- Gain the ability to handle criticism with grace.
- Feel more comfortable in unfamiliar situations.
- Help reduce social anxiety and fear of crowds.
- Overcome feelings of vulnerability and helplessness.
- Develop a sense of empowerment in your life.
- Improve confidence in your appearance.
- Overcome fear of speaking in front of others.
- Release feelings of guilt and shame holding back your confidence.
- Allow yourself to be more authentic and true to yourself.
- Overcome fear of success or fear of achieving goals.
- Break free from limiting beliefs that undermine confidence.
- Build confidence in social media and online interactions

- Help you accept and embrace compliments without discomfort.
- Enhance your ability to network and form meaningful relationships.
- Allow you to feel more comfortable in leadership positions.
- Build mental resilience to handle setbacks with confidence.
- Overcome fear of asking for help when needed.
- Cultivate a sense of inner calm and control during stressful situations.
- Increase your ability to trust your intuition and decision-making.
- Strengthen your ability to take calculated risks.
- Empower you to express your opinions and ideas openly.
- Boost your ability to say no without feeling guilty.
- Feel more at ease in job interviews and career advancement opportunities.
- Improve your body language to convey confidence to others.
- Release past failures that hinder confidence in new ventures.
- Strengthen your ability to recover from setbacks quickly.
- Develop an unwavering belief in your goals and aspirations.
- Overcome the fear of competing with others and embrace healthy competition.
- Help you feel more comfortable with making mistakes and learning from them.
- Support you in maintaining composure under pressure.
- Help you develop resilience when facing adversity.
- Increase your ability to perform in high-stress situations.
- Help you stop comparing yourself to others and focus on your own path.
- Boost confidence when taking on new challenges or responsibilities.
- Overcome shyness and social hesitation.
- Increase your capacity for self-compassion and self-love.
- Help you stop procrastinating due to a lack of confidence.
- Create a positive mindset that attracts success and opportunities.
- Encourage you to pursue goals without fear of the unknown.
- Help you embrace your unique qualities and strengths.
- Increase your self-reliance and independence.
- Build confidence in your decision-making abilities.
- Support you in letting go of the fear of the future.
- Enhance your ability to maintain focus and clarity in uncertain situations.
- Improve your relationships by boosting self-confidence.
- Empower you to ask for promotions or salary increases.
- Help you overcome feelings of inferiority.
- Improve your performance in competitive situations, such as exams or sports.
- Encourage you to take ownership of your actions and decisions.
- Help you stop apologizing for being yourself.
- Break through fears of public failure or humiliation.
- Help you navigate complex or difficult situations with confidence.

- Increase self-sufficiency and independence in everyday life.
- Overcome the fear of being judged for your choices.
- Build a deeper belief in your potential and talents.
- Help you feel confident in your creativity and originality.
- Release old, outdated beliefs that limit your ability to succeed.
- Improve your ability to relax and reduce anxiety in unfamiliar situations.
- Empower you to pursue personal growth and self-improvement.
- Allow you to communicate more confidently with others.
- Help you face and overcome your fears with courage.
- Help you create and maintain a growth mindset.
- Improve confidence in your ability to solve problems and overcome challenges.
- Increase self-reliance in making life-changing decisions.
- Enhance your ability to trust your gut feelings.
- Help you stop seeking validation from others and focus on your own beliefs.
- Boost your confidence in romantic relationships.
- Help you express your emotions clearly and without fear.
- Strengthen your ability to adapt to change with confidence.
- Help you develop an attitude of gratitude and positivity.
- Encourage you to focus on progress, not perfection.
- Build the courage to pursue long-term goals without hesitation.
- Improve your ability to maintain a positive self-talk cycle.
- Build self-confidence to pursue your passions and interests.
- Help you trust in the process and have faith in your journey.
- Support your personal development by eliminating self-imposed limitations.
- Encourage you to feel proud of your accomplishments.
- Strengthen your ability to stay calm and composed in challenging situations.
- Help you develop a strong internal sense of confidence.
- Build trust in your abilities to navigate the complexities of life.
- Enhance your ability to bounce back from failure with confidence.
- Help you move past past traumas that hinder your confidence.
- Encourage you to embrace challenges as opportunities for growth.
- Support you in creating a clear vision for your future.
- Help you step into leadership roles with ease and grace.
- Strengthen your ability to take initiative and lead projects.
- Support you in making decisions that align with your values and goals.
- Encourage you to move past fears of being perceived as "too much" or "too little."
- Increase your confidence in presenting new ideas or innovations.
- Develop a sense of inner strength to support your external confidence.
- Encourage you to take risks that will lead to personal growth.
- Help you to remain positive and confident in the face of challenges.

- Build your confidence to say "yes" to opportunities that challenge you.
- Help you view setbacks as temporary and surmountable.
- Develop an unshakable belief in your ability to succeed.
- Improve your confidence in building and maintaining professional relationships.
- Strengthen your resolve when faced with difficult decisions or choices.
- Help you embrace vulnerability as a strength, not a weakness.
- Empower you to step out of your comfort zone with confidence.
- Encourage you to trust in your unique path and journey.
- Help you celebrate your strengths rather than focusing on weaknesses.
- Support you in achieving balance between self-compassion and confidence.
- Increase your self-assurance in social or networking situations.
- Reinforce the belief that you are capable of achieving great things.
- Empower you to handle life's obstacles with resilience and confidence.
- Encourage you to keep moving forward even in the face of uncertainty.
- Build your self-belief by reframing negative experiences.
- Develop a consistent, positive inner dialogue that supports your goals.
- Help you increase your visibility in your career or personal life.
- Encourage you to pursue leadership roles and challenge the status quo.
- Allow you to feel proud of your achievements, both big and small.
- Help you to recognize and overcome self-sabotaging behaviors.
- Empower you to navigate social challenges with ease.
- Help you create and maintain a positive mindset despite setbacks.
- Encourage you to focus on your personal growth, not external validation.
- Boost your confidence to try new things and embrace unfamiliar experiences.
- Strengthen your ability to act confidently, even in the face of fear.
- Help you understand and embrace your worth as an individual.
- Support you in creating healthy habits that build long-term confidence.
- Encourage you to develop a strong sense of purpose and direction in life.
- Reinforce the belief that you are deserving of success and happiness.
- Help you transform past failures into stepping stones for future success.
- Strengthen your emotional intelligence to support your confidence.
- Empower you to let go of limiting beliefs that hold back your success.
- Help you become your own biggest supporter and cheerleader.
- Cultivate a belief that you have everything you need to succeed within you.
- Encourage you to view challenges as opportunities to learn and grow.
- Help you build resilience in the face of life's difficulties, fostering lasting confidence.

Have Questions / Comments?

This book was designed to cover as much as possible but I know I have probably missed something, or some new amazing discovery that has just come out.

If you notice something missing or have a question that I failed to answer, please get in touch and let me know. If I can, I will email you an answer and also update the book so others can also benefit from it.

Thanks For Being Awesome :)

Submit Your Questions / Comments At:

https://questions.xspurts.com

Get Another Book Free

We love writing and have produced a huge number of books.

For being one of our amazing readers, we would love to offer you another book we have created, 100% free.

To claim this limited time special offer, simply go to the site below and enter your name and email address.

You will then receive one of my great books, direct to your email account, 100% free!

https://free.xspurts.com

www.ingramcontent.com/pod-product-compliance
Lightning Source LLC
Chambersburg PA
CBHW061344250726
48657CB00004B/1329